DATE DUE

SEP 2 1 1995	JAN 0 7 1997	DEC 2 6 2006
	FEB 1 4 1997	FEB 1 5 2007
NOV 1 8 1995	MAR 0 1 1997	FEB 1 0 2012
JAN 0 8 1996	APR 2 1997	JUN 1 6 2012
	MAY 2 2 1996	AUG 0 7 2012
FEB 2 0 1996	JUN 2 8 1997	APR 6 2014
MAR 2 0 1996	MAR 1 9 2008	DEC 2 2 2015
JUN 1 3 1996	MAY 2 3 2002	FEB 1 2 2016
JUL 1 5 1996	MAR 1 9 2003	
NOV 2 0 1996	NOV 1 8 2003	
	APR 2 5 2006	

MAYA ANGELOU

GENIUS!
The Artist and the Process

MAYA ANGELOU

by
Nancy Shuker

GENIUS!
The Artist and the Process

SILVER BURDETT PRESS

Created and produced by: Blackbirch Graphics, Inc.

Project Editor: Emily Easton
Designer: Cynthia Minichino
Cover Design: Leslie Bauman

Manufactured in The United States of America

10   9   8   7   6   5   4   3   2

Library of Congress Cataloging-in-Publication Data
Shuker, Nancy.
    Maya Angelou / by Nancy Shuker.
    (Genius!: the artist and the process)
    Includes bibliographical references
    Summary: Portrays the life of the poet, musician, and actress, focusing on her struggles as a woman, as a mother, and as an artist.
    1. Angelou, Maya — Juvenile literature.   2. Authors, American — 20th century — Biography — Juvenile literature.   3. Entertainers — United States — Biography — Juvenile literature.   4. Afro-American woman authors — Biography — Juvenile literature.   [1. Angelou, Maya.   2. Authors, American.   3. Entertainers.   4. Afro-Americans — Biography.]   I. Title.   II. Series: Genius! (Englewood Cliffs, N.J.)   PS3551.N464Z88   1990   818'.5409—dc20 [B] [92]
    ISBN 0-382-09908-7 (lib. bdg.)   90-8497
    ISBN 0-382-240367 (pbg.)   CIP
                                                                                       AC.

Acknowledgments
Excerpt from "Lift Every Voice and Sing" by James Weldon Johnson used with permission of Edward B. Marks Music Co.
Excerpts from the "Oprah Winfrey Show" used by permission of Harpo Productions, Inc.
Excerpts from "A Second Look with Bill Moyers" used by permission of Public Affairs Television and Maya Angelou.
Excerpts from Maya Angelou's work used by permission of the author.

(Frontispiece)
Maya Angelou—a creative force in dance, drama, and literature.

Contents

It is the desperate traveler who teaches us the most profound lesson and affords us the most exquisite thrills. She touches us with her boldness and vulnerability, for her sole preparation is the fierce determination to leave where she is, and her only certain destination is somewhere other than where she has been.
—Maya Angelou

CHAPTER 1

WALK TOGETHER CHILDREN

More than 4,000 Moroccans jumped to their feet, screaming and shouting for more. Maya Angelou—age twenty-six, a poor, black girl from the American South—stood amazed.

She knew she was not a great singer. The audience was not applauding her great talent. In fact, when the orchestra conductor for the American production of *Porgy and Bess* had asked her to give a concert, she had declined, saying she was not an opera singer. "But you know spirituals," he insisted. Maya agreed to do the concert. After all, she had sung "Poor Pilgrim of Sorrow" and "Steal Away" and many other spirituals hundreds of times as a child in her grandmother's church in Stamps, Arkansas. She could sing them now.

But she had not known until the Moroccan audience went wild exactly what her people had given her. "I had a heritage," says Maya, "rich and nearer than the tongue which gave it voice. My mind resounded with the words and my blood raced to the rhythms." The black spirituals had sprung from an oppressed people to ease their pain. Today they are still a wellspring of solace and determination. Their message reaches beyond national borders, beyond languages, even beyond one religion.

The universal message that the spirituals carry had touched the Moroccans, but so too had the messenger. Although there is no description of Maya's perform-ance, we know that she has the ability to send audi-ences into rapture with her voice and delivery. When Maya sang that night in Morocco, she was singing her life. She understood what the words meant, and she was able to make her audience feel it.

As a black girl growing up in the United States in the 1920s and 1930s, Maya faced brutal racism and pov-erty. The Great Depression had thrown millions of people out of work. The prosperous suffered financial losses; the poor suffered unrelenting hardship.

Poverty was already a way of life for black people in the cotton-farming regions of the South where Maya and her brother lived with their grandmother. The pay for planting and picking the white man's crop in good times hardly covered the cost of a house. Most black families did not own their own land, so they worked other people's fields and paid rent for living quarters. Families ate from their own gardens, made over hand-me-down clothes, and limited store purchases to staples like flour and rice and products they couldn't make themselves, such as shoes for winter.

Apart from the physical hardship was the constant feeling that if you were black you were somehow inferior. Blacks, adults and children, faced daily humiliation and the threat that for one small violation of the unwritten white social code, their house could be burned down or they could be beaten or killed.

Maya was keenly aware that she was despised for the color of her skin. This was so painful for her that she would often imagine that she was white. In the first of her books about her life, *I Know Why the Caged Bird Sings*, she writes of how she felt as a black child:

> Wouldn't they be surprised when one day I woke out of my black ugly dream, and my real hair, which was long and blond, would take the place of the kinky mass....Because I was really white and because a cruel fairy stepmother, who was understandably jealous of my beauty, had turned me into a too-big Negro girl, with nappy black hair, broad feet and space between my teeth that would hold a number-two pencil.

Maya would struggle with this poor image of herself for many years. But from this painful and sometimes terrifying childhood, she has emerged as a self-confident woman with many gifts. She has been a dancer, actress, and singer. And now she is a novelist, poet, dramatist, and composer. In all of these artistic endeavors, Maya has been able to tell not only about the experience of black people but about the human experience. As she says, "I speak to the black experience, but I am always talking about the human condition— about what we can endure, dream, fail at, and still survive."

Marguerite Johnson was born in St. Louis, Missouri, in 1928, although shortly afterward her parents moved to California. She was called first "My" for "my sister" and then "Maya" by her brother, Bailey. Since he was the most important person in her young life, it was the name she liked best.

One of Maya's first memories is of being nestled into the seat of a train next to Bailey. She wore a tag on her

Picking cotton–an image common to Maya's early years in Stamps, Arkansas.

wrist that read "To Whom It May Concern—These children are Marguerite and Bailey Johnson, Jr., from Long Beach, California, en route to Stamps, Arkansas, c/o Mrs. Annie Henderson."

Maya was three years old. Her brother and protector, Bailey, was four. They had been put on the train by their father, who was sending them home to his mother. His marriage to their mother was over and shipping them to their grandmother was the only way he could think of to take care of them.

In the 1930s in the United States, black children were regularly tagged and shipped by train back and forth between parents in northern and western cities and grandparents in the rural South. Parents, discouraged by the poverty and racism of their home towns, went to large cities to find new and better work opportunities. If they succeeded, they sent for their children. When things went bad, they shipped the youngsters back to grandparents in the country.

Maya's Grandmother Henderson owned a store in Stamps, which served lunch as well as selling a wide variety of merchandise. The sign over the store read "Wm. Johnson General Merchandise Store." William Johnson was Maya and Bailey's grandfather, but they never met him. He had left their grandmother with two small boys to raise early in the 1900s, and he had not been heard of since. Although their grandmother had married again, first to a Mr. Henderson and then to a Mr. Murphy, each man abandoned her. After bearing her sons, she had no more children.

Modest quarters at the rear of the store became the children's home and the center of their lives. Maya shared a bed with her grandmother and Bailey doubled up with Uncle Willie, their father's brother, who was a cripple. The store was lighted by coal-oil lamps when the children first came to live there and water was brought up in buckets from the well out back. The children went down to the well to wash themselves with soap and cold water every night before bed—no matter what the weather—and their toilet was in an outhouse. In winter a wood-burning stove warmed the store for customers and the family.

Momma, as she quickly came to be called, had no patience with uppity children. Maya and Bailey were taught to address adults as ma'am or sir or to call them Mr. or Mrs. or Sister or Brother with their last names. If they were asked a question, the answer was not "yes" or "no." It was "yes, ma'am" or "no, sir." Although she was very strict with them, Maya and Bailey felt their grandmother's love and protection.

They also sensed her protective love for the whole black community. At cotton-picking time, the farm owners brought their trucks to the store to pick up the day workers, who were expected to be in the fields from dawn to dark. Maya later described how her grandmother would get up at four A.M., say her prayers, and then wake the children to help her open the store for the workers, who would have walked in from the surrounding countryside. They wore overalls and carried long oval bags that hung across their chests to carry the white tufts of cotton they would tear off the sharp bolls that held them tight to the plant. In the pale morning light, the men joked and bragged about how much they could pick as they bought their lunch food to take with them. At night they were exhausted and discouraged, knowing that despite their stooped backs and sore fingers, they hadn't made their optimistic quotas. And yet, with only a few hours of sleep, the next morning they would start all over again, bantering with the top picker of the day before. Momma knew that many of them would never be able to settle their bills with the store.

As the Depression worsened, the price of cotton fell and the workers were paid even less. The county welfare agency gave food to poor families, black and white. These provisions included lard, flour, salt, powdered eggs, and powdered milk.

The Hendersons were among the few black families not on welfare, but the store could not survive if none of its customers paid. Momma borrowed one of the children's school tablets and started doing figures at night after supper. She came up with a solution and called them in to help her. Bailey's job was to letter a large sign. Maya's job was to color it with her crayons. The sign carefully spelled out the value in trade of each food item given out by the welfare agencies. A five-pound can of powdered milk, for example, was worth fifty cents in trade. A five-pound can of powdered eggs was worth one dollar. The system worked and both the store and the community survived.

Religion played an important part in Maya's early life. She and Bailey were expected to distinguish themselves in Sunday school as well as lead Christian lives. Momma's active support of the Christian Meth-

People looked to the typical general store in the South for everything they couldn't make themselves.

odist Episcopal Church in Stamps included attendance at services every Sunday.

A soft-spoken woman, Annie Henderson found her voice in church, where she was regularly asked to lead the congregation in the hymn. The young Maya was always startled by the strength and vigor of her grandmother's singing in church. As an adult Maya would draw strength and wisdom from these old songs of worship. They were admired by white people as Negro spirituals, but to Maya they were the shared heritage of her black childhood. The cadences and melodies of the old songs would show up repeatedly in her poetry.

Maya was a lanky, self-conscious child, who thought her brother's wiry grace and easy athleticism were physical perfection. Not knowing what her parents looked like didn't help. A part of her suspected that they, too, were beautiful like Bailey and that she didn't really belong to them.

Certainly, it never occurred to her that there was any connection between her own colt-like physique and her grandmother's stately dignity, which she greatly admired. Her grandmother, just short of six feet, was the tallest woman Maya had ever seen. But height was not something she could discuss with Momma. Momma worried about God and goodness, not looks. Only as an adult, having traveled halfway around the world to Africa where she discovered a tribe in which the women were all very tall, would Maya come to recognize the heritage she shared with her handsome grandmother.

Maya and Bailey lived securely in Stamps for three years before their lives were interrupted. It started with two packages that arrived in the mail for them just in time for Christmas. One was from their mother and one was from their father.

In 1936, many southern blacks lived on small cotton patches.

Maya and Bailey did not remember anything about California. Nor did they really remember their parents. It was a subject neither child liked to talk about— even between themselves. They each privately assumed that their parents had sent them away because they were somehow not good enough to be kept. They

Modest black churches such as this served as the center of the
black community.

felt terribly guilty about their obvious inadequacies.
Maya later wrote that she wanted so badly to believe
that her mother was dead—which would explain why
she had allowed the children to be taken away from
her—that Maya imagined her beautiful mother in a
coffin.

Surprise packages normally are an exciting event for
children. But Maya was filled with dread even before

she was allowed to open the gifts. She didn't discuss it with Bailey then. She was too upset. If their parents, after three years, were suddenly sending them presents, it meant that their mother and father were not dead. And if they were not dead, then they really must be angry at the children. Otherwise, why would they have sent Maya and Bailey to Stamps and not written to them for three years?

Opening the presents on Christmas morning didn't make Maya feel any better. Their father sent a photograph of himself. He was a good-looking man, which gave Maya further proof that she was not really a member of the family. Their mother sent her a tea set and a blond, blue-eyed, white doll. Maya was aghast. Did her mother want a blond, blue-eyed white child instead of Maya? She, of course, could not have known that black dolls were not an item that white toy manufacturers featured in those days.

Maya and Bailey tore all the stuffing out of her doll the day after Christmas. Afterward, Bailey had second thoughts. Maybe the reason they had received gifts from their parents was that they had been very angry with the children, but now they were beginning to forgive them and would come get them. He told Maya to take care of the tea set because their mother might ride up any day.

As it turned out, it wasn't their mother who came to get them. It was their father. Maya recalls, "It was awful for Bailey and me to encounter the reality one abrupt morning. We, or at any rate I, had built such elaborate fantasies about him and the illusory mother that seeing him in the flesh shredded my inventions like a hard yank on a paper chain."

Their father, Bailey, Sr., was the tallest man Maya had ever seen. His shoulders were so broad she questioned their fitting through the front door of Momma's store. He wore a tight-fitted suit and spoke English like the school principal. Maya's first impression was that he was "blindingly handsome."

She was torn between feelings of pride and a feeling that he might indeed be Bailey's father, but he couldn't be hers or she would be prettier. She decided that she was an orphan her parents had picked up to keep Bailey company.

Maya and Bailey basked in the light of their father's celebrity for three weeks. He entertained the continuous stream of people who came to visit him in the store, and Momma bustled around cooking all her best dishes for him. Everyone wanted to check in with the local brother who had made good. No one—certainly not Maya and Bailey—had any idea what he really did for a living. At the time of his visit to Stamps, he was working in the kitchen of a Naval base in San Diego.

It soon became clear that Bailey Sr. was going to take the children with him. Bailey Jr. was ecstatic at the idea. Maya had reservations, but she didn't know how to discuss them with Momma. Nor did she know how Momma felt about it. She became resigned to the trip.

The assumption was that they were going to California. It was not until they were in the car heading west that they were told their real destination. They were being delivered to their mother and her family in St. Louis, where she had returned after splitting up with Bailey, Sr.

The children were delivered to their mother, Vivian Baxter, at her parents' house on Caroline Street in St. Louis. Upon meeting her mother, Maya was, as she put it later, "struck dumb." She understood immediately why she and Bailey had been sent away. Their mother was simply too beautiful to have children.

Life in St. Louis was very different from life in Stamps. It was a throbbing, noisy, and bustling city, and Maya would later describe the black part of town as being like a gold-rush community where there was lots of money and very little law. Numbers runners, lottery takers, whiskey salesmen, and gamblers openly practiced their trades, and the school children all knew their names: Hard-Hitting Jimmy, Sweet Man, Two Gun, Poker Pete.

Bailey loved Vivian instantly and unreservedly. All the pain of their separation melted away as soon as he saw her. She was his Mother Dear. Maya understood when she saw them together. She felt that they were more alike than she and her mother could ever be or even more alike than she and Bailey were. They shared a physical grace and quirks of personality that she could appreciate.

City life was also easier for Bailey than for Maya. The soot, the noise, the smells, and the crowds were frightening to her. At their new school, which was housed in a building bigger than the white schools in Stamps, they found their classmates were far behind them in every subject, and the teachers were aloof and uncaring.

Maya and Bailey moved apart from each other in St. Louis. Bailey pursued his passion for sandlot ball games and schoolyard scrapping. Maya retreated to the place that gave her the most solace—the world of the imagination, books. During this time she writes,

> I spent most of my Saturdays at the library…breathing in the world of penniless shoeshine boys who, with goodness and perseverance, became rich, rich men, and gave baskets of goodies to the poor on holidays. The little princesses who were mistaken for maids…became more real to me than our house, our mother, our school….

The children lived at the Baxters' house for six months. Since Vivian worked in bars at night cutting

St. Louis in the late 1930s was a vibrant city in sharp contrast to small-town life in the South.

the cards for poker games, they saw very little of her. Sometimes after school she would invite them to visit her at a bar where she worked. Those afternoons were magic.

Bailey and Maya would slip in the back door of the bar. Vivian's friends would greet them and sit them down in a booth where they were served soft drinks and boiled shrimp. Then Vivian would pick out a record on the jukebox. When the music came on, she would dance for them. Sometimes she sang with the record. Maya thought she was like a pretty kite floating right out of their reach. She knew that everyone in the bar, including the owners, thought her mother the most beautiful and graceful woman in the world.

It was during these afternoons with her mother that dance grabbed Maya's interest. The first dance Vivian taught the children was the Time Step, a series of taps, jumps, and rests that must strike just the right beat in the music to work. The Time Step is basic to American black dancing.

Bailey learned the step with ease. Maya found it harder. "But," she writes, "I learned too. I approached the Time Step with the same determination to win that I approached the times tables with." She concentrated on the music. She taught herself to hear and feel the rhythm that determined the sequence of the dance step.

This tenaciousness flowed through Maya's life and would eventually turn into the bedrock of her creative being. Each challenge she faced would be like learning the Time Step. She would grind away at the challenge until she had conquered it.

Her mother and her mother's friends applauded Maya's dancing. She glowed at the attention, never dreaming that she would know the joy of dancing well and would be paid for doing it.

Vivian moved into an apartment with a man friend and took the children with her. The move didn't change their lives very much. They stayed in the same school and spent their free time in much the same way. Vivian went out in the late afternoon, and they were expected to eat their dinner, wash up the dishes, and do their homework before they listened to the radio or read.

Mr. Freeman, Vivian's man friend, worked at the railroad yards and usually came home after Maya and Bailey had eaten. He would take his dinner off the back of the stove where Vivian had left it, eat, and then sink into a living room chair to wait for her. He wasn't rude to the children; he just didn't pay much attention to them.

Maya didn't pay much attention to Mr. Freeman either until he sexually abused her one morning. He told her that if she mentioned to anyone what he had done, he would kill Bailey. Maya was horrified. She had never kept a secret from Bailey in her whole life. But she could not imagine life without Bailey, so she kept still.

Life went on as it had before for a while. Mr. Freeman paid no attention to Maya at all. So it was surprising to her one Saturday morning when Vivian was not home that he should ask her to go to the store to get milk for his coffee and bring it back before going to the library.

Maya did as she was told. But when she returned to the apartment, Mr. Freeman didn't have coffee on his mind. He grabbed Maya and raped her. Shocked and hurting, she was unable to walk. Again Mr. Freeman threatened to kill Bailey if she told anyone. Vivian found her daughter in bed with a fever and thought she was coming down with the measles. It was several hours before she learned what had happened and took Maya to the hospital.

Charges were brought against Freeman, and at the trial Maya had to testify. The way the questions were asked, she felt that she had to lie about the first incident with Mr. Freeman to save Bailey. She knew Mr. Freeman would know that she had lied, and she hated sharing a secret with him. She also believed that God, hearing her lie, would withhold his grace from her.

Mr. Freeman was found guilty and was sentenced to a year in prison, but he never served the sentence. Maya and Bailey were playing Monopoly in their grandmother's parlor when a white policeman came to report that Freeman had been found dead in the lot behind the slaughterhouse. The policeman said he had been kicked to death.

Maya was sure that her mother's relatives had killed Mr. Freeman. She was also sure that her lie in the courtroom, which she told to protect Bailey, was connected to the man's death.

She later wrote "... a man was dead because I lied. Where was the balance in that? One lie surely wouldn't be worth a man's life....I could feel the evilness flowing through my body and waiting, pent up, to rush off my tongue if I tried to open my mouth....If it escaped, wouldn't it flood the world and all the innocent people?" In her mind she saw that her talking caused people to die. She became afraid to talk to anyone but Bailey (she believed that her ferocious love for him would protect him).

The family was sympathetic for a while, but when silent months had passed and Maya still refused to talk, they lost patience. She and Bailey were sent back to Momma in Stamps.

The rhythms and spirituals of the African-American church
service formed a strong imprint on young Maya.

CHAPTER 2

A PILGRIM OF SORROW

Lying, thinking
Last night
How to find my soul a home
Where water is not thirsty
And bread loaf is not stone
I came up with one thing
And I don't believe I'm wrong
That nobody,
But nobody
Can make it out here alone.
—Maya Angelou
From the poem, "Alone"

Maya's silence came from fear and guilt, but in an odd way it also taught her how to listen, a talent she would later draw upon as a writer. "I discovered," she writes, "that to find perfect personal silence, all I had to do was to attach myself leechlike to sound. I began to listen to everything. I probably hoped that after I had heard all the sounds, really heard them and packed them down, deep in my ears, the world would be quiet around me." But Maya's world was not quiet, and she absorbed and stored away the sounds.

The church's sounds were among these. She soaked up the repetitive rhythms and cadence of the preacher's sermons, the congregation's responses, and, of course, the spirituals. The music soothed her, but it was the words that gave her even greater comfort.

"Always in the black spirituals there's that promise," she says, "that things are going to be better, by and by...." The same rich language is threaded throughout her writing.

Her voracious reading also continued and fed her internal imaginary world. She would often imagine taking tea with English ladies in mansions on the moors. It didn't matter that she had never heard of "hot tea" (in the South there was only "iced tea") or had never set foot in a mansion or seen a moor. She was captivated by the words and the descriptions in these books, and especially by the "music." She writes, "When I read Shakespeare and heard that music, I couldn't believe it, that a white man could write so musically. I already... had an affection for [Edgar Allan] Poe, because I like his rhythm. I like 'Then, upon that velvet sinking, I betook myself to thinking fancy unto fancy, linking,' it's marvelous, it's rhythmic."

These sounds were kept tightly locked in Maya's head. No whisper passed her lips until Mrs. Bertha Flowers came along and opened the flood gates of Maya's speech. Maya greatly admired Mrs. Flowers, who was a close friend of her grandmother. She was an educated woman who lived alone in a small house up the hill from the store. She was, according to Maya, "the aristocrat of Black Stamps." She had a grace that made her always seem cool and collected, even in the hottest weather. She wore flowered hats and sheer print dresses that suited her as well as overalls suited the local farmers. Maya thought she was like the gracious white women in the English novels. "She was our side's answer to the richest white woman in town," Maya writes. "She was one of the few gentlewomen I have ever known, and has remained throughout my life the measure of what a human being can be."

When Mrs. Flowers came into the store, Maya marveled that such a lady would have so much to say to her grandmother. Maya winced when she heard Momma use incorrect grammar in conversation with Mrs. Flowers. It didn't seem to bother Mrs. Flowers. The two would sit and chat for long periods. Maya was amazed that this cultivated person could find anything in common with her ignorant grandmother.

One day Mrs. Flowers came into the store, and asked if Maya could carry her groceries up the hill for her. That day is still "sweet-milk fresh" in Maya's memory. Mrs. Flowers's house turned out to be just as wonderful to Maya as its owner. White lace curtains hung in the windows, and the smell of vanilla wafted through the living room.

Mrs. Flowers said that she had wanted to have a chat with Maya, so she had baked some tea cookies for her guest. As they drank cold lemonade and ate cookies, Mrs. Flowers started talking to Maya about some of the books she loved. She read aloud some of her favorite passages.

She showed Maya her library and told Maya that she would happily lend books to her. There was one condition: in return, she wanted Maya to come and read aloud to her from the books Maya liked best. Maya was overcome with pleasure. This remarkable woman not only had made cookies just for her, now she wanted Maya to come back again and read to her. Maya remembers Mrs. Flowers telling her, "Words mean more than what is set down on paper. It takes the human voice to infuse them with shades of deeper meaning."

Little by little, without even being aware of it, Maya began talking naturally again. Mrs. Flowers had eased the troubled girl through her trauma with the beauty and power of written words shared aloud. She made

Maya appreciate the spoken word, a gift that Maya would continue to cultivate as an adult. Today, Maya Angelou mesmerizes audiences when she reads her own writing and the works of other black writers. Hearing her read a poem of his before an audience in New York in 1988, photographer, filmmaker, composer, and writer Gordon Parks looked into the auditorium with amazement. "It was like a new poem," he said.

Maya and Mrs. Flowers talked about the ideas behind the words they read to each other, and Maya came to understand why Mrs. Flowers and her grandmother were such good friends. It had to do with the difference between illiteracy, not having the benefit of an education, and ignorance, not seeing what was going on around you. Momma, Maya had to acknowledge, was not ignorant.

Momma tried to protect her grandchildren from the pain and cruelty of racism in Stamps. But it was impossible to shield them from it totally. When they were very young, they heard the sheriff ride up to warn Momma that the Klan was riding that night, and she better hide Uncle Willie.

The Ku Klux Klan, the children discovered, was a group of white men who put on costumes that looked like white sheets and at night terrorized black people, often dragging them out of their homes and hanging them, a practice known as lynching. Lynching was a common occurrence in the South. Thousands of blacks had been hanged or burned at the stake (between 1889 and 1921, 3,436 killings had been documented). Little had been done to stop this violence by the time Maya and Bailey were living in Stamps.

The Klan didn't appear to need much of an excuse to ride. If they thought a black person had been "uppity" or had offended a white person in some way, they

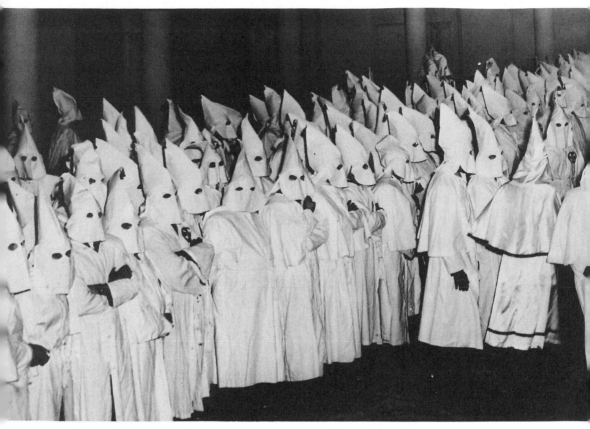

The Ku Klux Klan, an organization of white racists, terrorized blacks living in the South.

simply went after that individual or some other black person to "teach them a lesson." The lesson seemed to be that black people lived only by the grace of white people, and that privilege could be taken away at any time if black people weren't careful. Evidently the sheriff thought enough of their grandmother to warn her of the Klan's coming, but Maya didn't feel grateful. She thought the sheriff ought to stop the Klan from doing such terrible things.

Maya and Bailey helped clear out the potato bin in the store and, after Uncle Willie had crouched inside, they covered him over as well as they could. He spent an uncomfortable night there. The Klan never came, but Maya never got over her anger that Uncle Willie had to hide from them.

Aside from the constant fear, humiliation was a part of everyday life for blacks in the United States. In the South especially, black people lived, as one writer puts it, "behind a seemingly impenetrable wall of segregation...." They could not go into white public restrooms, drink from public drinking fountains, or do a thousand other things that people now take for granted. One incident in Maya's life shows this wall clearly.

Maya developed a tooth infection. Momma tried all her home remedies, but the pain and swelling persisted. Maya was in agony. The nearest black dentist was twenty-five miles away in Texarcana, Arkansas. Momma dressed Maya carefully and took her by the

Before the civil rights movement, separate public facilities were one of the indignities of life in the South.

hand into the white section of Stamps to the office of a white dentist. Momma knew him because he had borrowed money from her during the early years of the Depression. The loan, which he paid back without interest, had saved his practice. She assumed that he would return a favor.

Maya cringed when he addressed her grandmother as Annie. He refused to treat Maya. "Annie," he said, "my policy is I'd rather stick my hands in a dog's mouth than a nigger's." Momma took Maya outside and told her to wait and then returned to the office alone. Mrs. Henderson reminded the dentist in private that he owed her some interest if not a favor. After signing a paper absolving him of any further obligation, she had to accept $10. It was his final offer. But she still had to get help for her granddaughter. After a long bus ride, Maya's tooth was treated in Texarcana.

White society pushed down on Maya's psyche like a solid steel weight. She was aware of "the cage" around her. She would beat her wings against the bars valiantly, often only injuring herself. She writes of this awareness, "If growing up is painful for the Southern Black girl, being aware of her displacement is the rust on the razor that threatens the throat. It is an unnecessary insult."

The racial hatred that Maya felt directed at her sunk deep emotional wounds that prevented her from trusting a white person or seeing who she really was until she was in her twenties.

Maya marveled at the resiliency of her people in the face of such unfairness. She had seen exhausted workers come back to the store at sundown, stooped and dragging from the cotton fields but eager to attend a tent revival meeting that same night.

The hymn singing in church or at the revival tent— not unlike the blues sung in cafés and bars—relieved

the pain and frustration of daily life. The lovely voices
blended in rich harmony. Maya, who one day would
write a musical review and the score for her own
movie, received her musical education singing in
church with her grandmother.

The community of the black church, its rich spiritual-
ism and comfort, sustained poor black people from
week to week in southern towns and cities. No matter
how bad things got at work or at home, black people
were safe in church and among friends who understood how hard life could be. A young black man
from Atlanta, Georgia, a year younger than Maya,
would tap this same power to mobilize black southern-
ers to political action. His name was Dr. Martin Luther
King, Jr., and one of his deputies in that church-based
battle for civil rights would be Maya Angelou.

As Maya healed from her St. Louis trauma, she
embraced the life of a school girl in Stamps. She made
a best friend with whom she could share secrets, and
she began to enjoy the church socials and picnics that
were entertainment in a small town.

She particularly looked forward to her graduation
from elementary school, which in Arkansas went
through eighth grade. Momma had worked for weeks
on her graduation dress, which included smocking,
puffed sleeves, and crocheted collar and cuffs.

Graduation from eighth grade for many black children was as important as graduating from high school.
It might be the end of their schooling if their parents
needed them to help support the family. In fact, a
number of black teachers in the elementary school only
had eighth-grade diplomas.

It was a milestone in young people's lives and was
celebrated by all the family. Momma and Uncle Willie
gave Maya a watch. The minister's wife had made the
petticoat she wore with her graduation dress. And

Maya Angelou

A PICTURE PORTFOLIO

Maya Angelou—actress, journalist, teacher, and author.

In the opening of the TV-series "Roots," Maya Angelou, as the grandmother of baby Kunte Kinte, watches with joy a birth not yet darkened by the shadow of slavery.

(*At right*)
A portrait of Maya Angelou by artist Spencer Lawrence, 1990.

Maya Angelou—a strong voice of the African-American experience.

A PICTURE PORTFOLIO

In the television adaptation of *I Know Why the Caged Bird Sings,*
Esther Rolle (left) played Grandma Henderson and Constance
Good played young Maya.

Bailey had saved for months to buy her a leatherbound
copy of Edgar Allen Poe's poems. They read "Anna-
belle Lee" together the morning of graduation.

Everyone at the school had worked on the festivities.
The younger children had prepared a play, the older
ones had made the refreshments. Momma even had
Bailey make a sign for the store that read "Closed.
Graduation." They hung it on the door as they left for
the school.

Maya didn't even mind that she had not been se-
lected valedictorian and would not be making a
speech. The young man who was given this honor was
her greatest rival in school, but he was someone she
admired. He, too, was raised by his grandmother, who
was just as strict as Momma, and he was a model
youngster around adults. But he was also as reckless
and daring on the playing field as Bailey, and that
made Maya appreciate him.

The speaker of the day was a white man from the state education department in Little Rock. He rushed onto the stage because, as the school principal explained, he didn't have much time and he had to "speak and run."

The white man looked at his audience once and then read from a sheaf of papers. He wanted to tell them all the wonderful things that were happening to improve education in their community. A famous artist from Little Rock was coming to Stamps to teach art. New microscopes had been ordered and new equipment for the chemistry lab. Of course all these things were for the white high school, not for them. But they were not being left out, he said, because they were to have the first paved playing field in their part of the state.

The man was not telling parents and students anything that was surprising. In the 1930s and 1940s, when Maya was attending school, most southern states were spending between five and ten times more money on white students than on black students. Schools for black children were unheated cabins and tarpaper shacks, while white schools were tidy brick and stone buildings with well-heated, well-lighted classrooms. The man was just telling them the truth.

Maya knew this, but she still ached for her classmates who showed so much promise in all the subjects that the official had dismissed as not relevant for black students. His message was clear—blacks were only good in sports. No one had any intellectual expectations for them.

The white speaker left the stage and the school as soon as he had finished. His stunned audience sat in an ugly silence as the young valedictorian stood up to speak. His prepared text—rewritten and practiced weeks beforehand—was based on Hamlet's "To be or not to be" soliloquy. Maya thought sourly to herself that obviously black people could not hope to "be" anything, so there was no point in asking the question. It was difficult for Maya to even listen to the speech under the circumstances. It was too painful to watch her friend, so she closed her eyes.

Suddenly he stopped speaking, and when Maya looked, he had turned to his fellow classmates, the proud graduates of 1940, and was asking them to join him in singing James Weldon Johnson's hymn "Lift Every Voice and Sing."

> Lift ev'ry voice and sing
> Till earth and heaven ring
> Ring with the harmonies of Liberty . . .

Slowly the class began to join in.

> Stony the road we trod
> Bitter the chastening rod
> Felt in the days when hope, unborn, had died.
> Yet with a steady beat
> Have not our weary feet
> Come to the place for which our father sighed?

Parents stood and sang with their children.

> We have come over a way that with tears has been watered,
> We have come, treading our path through the blood of the
>   slaughtered.
> Out from the gloomy past
> Till now we stand at last
> Where the white gleam of our bright star is cast.

The singing of what many blacks consider to be their national anthem put a cool salve on the stinging wound. The shared hurt, expressed together in the well-loved words and music, made a community of the parents, teachers, and children that could not be destroyed by an insensitive white man from the Arkansas Department of Education.

Downtown San Francisco in the early 1940s.

CHAPTER 3

STREETWISE

*I was a loose kite in
a gentle wind
floating with only
my will for an
anchor.*
—Maya Angelou

Momma had tried to protect Maya and Bailey
from racism as much as possible by keeping them
away from the white section of Stamps, but no adult
can insulate a child's life forever.

Shortly after Maya's graduation from eighth grade,
Bailey was pulled into a racial incident that would
change his and Maya's life. As he made his way home
one afternoon from errands in the white part of town,
Bailey was drawn into a terrible scene. The police, all
of whom were white, were recovering the body of a
black man who had drowned in the Stamps pond.
They insisted that Bailey help some other black men
carry the bloated corpse to the jail. On closer inspec-
tion, Bailey realized that the man had not just

drowned; he had been badly mutilated first. At the jail, the police joked that they were going to lock Bailey and the other men in with the corpse. Bailey, who was thirteen, was shocked by the sight of the deteriorated, maimed body and even more shocked by the attitude of the police. The vicious death of a black man was a joke to them.

When Bailey finally got back to the store, he couldn't talk. Uncle Willie, who started to berate him for being late, recognized that something had happened and called Momma. Maya watched the scene wide-eyed. When Bailey could talk, he wailed at his grandmother and uncle, "Why do they hate us so much? What did we ever do to them?" It was the unanswerable question. Neither she nor Uncle Willie could give real comfort to Bailey because there wasn't any.

Maya always believed that Bailey's incident with the police inspired Momma's decision to return her grandchildren to their parents in California, where they might have a chance in life that they would never have in Stamps. Whatever the reason, it was shortly after Bailey's experience that Momma began preparations for the trip. To afford the train fares, she bartered with friends who worked on the railroad: for a pass on the train for herself, she gave grocery credits at the store. She would have to put up cash for Maya and Bailey's tickets.

Momma, who had never been farther than Texarcana in her life, set off to settle her grandchildren in California. Since Bailey, Sr. was in Southern California, Momma made Los Angeles her destination. Vivian had settled with her widowed mother and two of her brothers in Oakland, near San Francisco. She came down to meet Momma and help her find an apartment. Maya marveled at how her country grandmother coped with life in the city amidst her

Mexican and Asian neighbors. First, of course, she found a church, and soon women from the congregation were coming for Sunday supper, just as they did in Stamps.

Bailey, Sr. visited them sporadically but seemed unable to make definite plans for his children. After several months of negotiations, it was Vivian who arranged to make a home for them with her. Maya was still amazed by her mother's beauty and natural grace, but she had reservations about living with her again. St. Louis was still a very bad memory for Maya. Momma was anxious to return to Stamps to take care of Uncle Willie and the store. If she had asked Maya to go back with her, Maya would have gone gladly. Even without Bailey, she later wrote, she would have accompanied Momma home, but Momma never asked her.

After a brief stint with her Baxter relatives (Maya shared a bed with Grandmother Baxter, who smoked cigarettes all night in between coughing spells), the children moved into a house in San Francisco with Vivian and her new husband, whom Maya and Bailey called Daddy Clidell. Maya chose to ignore Daddy Clidell.

She was miserable in the first school she was enrolled in. It was an all-girls' school near where they lived. The black and Hispanic student population was from families like hers that were new to San Francisco, but they had come from more sophisticated cities than Stamps, and the youngsters were tougher and more streetwise than Maya (they carried knives in their hair) and were far less interested in their studies.

Vivian eventually enrolled Maya in George Washington High School, which was more academically demanding. The school was located in a white residential area of the city, and Maya had to take a long bus ride to get there. In the beginning, she was one of only three black students. Maya discovered right away that being the number two student in Stamps didn't give her any status in George Washington High School. She had to work hard just to keep up. The white students had larger vocabularies than Maya, and they were much less afraid to speak up in class.

Although many teachers tried to be kind to her because she was black, it was her social studies teacher, Miss Kirwin, who seemed to be color blind, that Maya loved best. Miss Kirwin treated every student alike and asked only that they keep up with the news and use their minds to think. She had no favorites. Each day was a fresh start, and each student was judged on the quality of his or her arguments about issues of the day. Maya sensed the teacher's reverence for knowledge and responded wholeheartedly. Her classes were the highlight of Maya's day.

In the evenings, after dinner with Bailey and Vivian, Maya took drama and modern dance classes at the California Labor School, where she was the youngest student. Somehow Vivian had arranged a scholarship for her.

Maya's drama classes had a rough start. Her drama experience came from watching the preacher wail out his Sunday sermons and reading Shakespeare aloud with her brother. This, along with her own active imagination and forceful personality, made her acting melodramatic at best, which did not go over well with her drama teacher.

> It was hard to curb my love for the exaggerated gesture and the emotive voice. When Bailey and I read poems together, he sounded like a fierce Basil Rathbone and I like a maddened Bette Davis. At the California Labor School a forceful and perceptive teacher quickly and unceremoniously separated me from melodrama. She made me do six months of pantomime.

Maya enjoyed drama, but it was dance that caught her whole heart. She writes that "when the teacher floated across the floor and finished in an arabesque my fancy was taken." She was determined to become a dancer.

The Japanese attacked Pearl Harbor on December 7, 1941, bringing the United States into World War II. Maya heard the news on the street and ran home, not quite sure if the family was in imminent danger of being bombed.

The war brought opportunities for black people in San Francisco. Jobs in defense factories paid better wages for men and women than many country people had ever dreamed of. The black population swelled with soldiers, sailors, factory workers, and opportunity seekers who saw an easy living to be made from the influx of new people with ready cash.

Vivian and Daddy Clidell filled their house with boarders from this new economy, including a number of nightclub dancers who fascinated Maya with their heavy makeup and outrageous clothes. They were exotic creatures to her. She never saw that they were girls only a few years older than she with far less education.

Vivian attracted an array of admirers from her nightclub and after-hours world—successful gamblers and petty racketeers who were colorful and entertaining. They wore zoot suits—broad-shouldered jackets with wide lapels that tapered to the hip over baggy pants—and lots of gold chains. They had cash in their pockets, and they knew how to have a good time.

Daddy Clidell had done pretty well for himself as a businessman. He had grown up poor in the rural South and had to quit school early to work in the field. He never pretended to have had an education. Nor did he make a special point of his accomplishments,

San Francisco had a seamy side replete with night clubs and cheap hotels.

which he attributed to luck, hard work, and being fair to the people who worked for him. He was a man who was comfortable with himself. In spite of her reservations about her own father and her terrible experience with Mr. Freeman, Maya slowly warmed to Daddy Clidell. She respected his honesty and his lack of pretensions.

It was about this time that Maya began getting a different kind of education—one that would be destructive and painful at times but that would also give her an understanding of human nature and society.

Many of Daddy's friends who came to the house were successful con men. They made their living tricking other people out of their money. They loved to entertain each other—and Maya—with stories of how they had set up their victims, whom they referred to as their "marks." They took particular relish in describing in detail how they had swindled white men. They used to assure Maya that the con game did have morals. No mark, they emphasized to her, ever falls for a con unless he is so greedy that he deludes himself into thinking he can get something for nothing. Smart people know better, they told her.

Maya says that she began to see how people who are kept on the fringes of society, who are not allowed to participate fully, survive. The con men and gamblers who were a part of her daily life, she writes, "used their intelligence to pry open the door of rejection and not only become wealthy but got some revenge in the bargain." These people were using the only means open to them. "The needs of society," she explains, "determine its ethics, and in the black American ghettos the hero is the man who is offered only crumbs from his country's table but by ingenuity and courage is able to take for himself...a feast."

Another part of Maya's so-called street education had to do with learning another language. It was not a language that was taught in any school. It was spoken in the street, among the people. Maya's ear was attuned to its sound and structure. "In the classroom," she writes, "we all learned past participles, but in the streets and in our homes the Blacks learned to drop s's from plurals and suffixes from past-tense verbs....We learned to slide out of one language and into another...." Maya's ability to "slide" in and out of different ways of artistic expression, like her ability to use different ways of speaking, would serve her well when she began to explore her creative self.

Yet another educational experience awaited Maya in Southern California. Bailey, Sr. invited her to spend her summer vacation with him and his girlfriend, Dolores, in Long Beach. Maya was looking forward to being with her father and seeing the sights around Los Angeles. Unfortunately, she walked into a hornet's nest instead. Dolores and Bailey were not a happy couple. She desperately wanted to marry him, and he had little use for her.

Bailey, Sr. also had little interest in showing his daughter a good time while she was there. So Maya was surprised when he offered to take her to Mexico, supposedly to buy authentic ingredients for a Mexican dinner. She was excited about seeing another country and trying out her high school Spanish.

The trip and the aftermath were disastrous. Bailey ignored Maya when they reached Mexico and proceeded to get drunk. Maya ended up using her minimal language skills to get his comatose body into the car and then driving the car to the border (her first experience at the wheel). When they finally arrived home, Dolores was furious that she had not been invited to go along. She took her fury out on Maya. When she insulted Vivian, Maya slapped her. In the struggle that followed, Dolores managed to stab Maya. When Bailey, Sr. awoke from his stupor, Maya was locked in a car, her side bleeding, and Dolores was circling the car with a hammer in her hand.

Bailey, Sr., fearing a scandal might jeopardize his standing with the naval base, took Maya to a friend's house for treatment. The woman washed out the wound, which proved to be superficial, and applied a bandage. Bailey then left Maya with other friends in the trailer park. He visited her briefly the next day but offered no future plans for either of them.

So Maya made her own plans. While her hosts were away at work, she made herself two tuna sandwiches, emptied their cupboard of bandages to change the dressing on her wound, and set off for town. After wandering around for most of the day, she arrived at a junkyard of abandoned cars she had spotted earlier. She climbed into a wheelless, gray hulk that still had floorboards. That it had a floor seemed an important protection against rats to her. She ate her sandwiches and fell asleep.

She woke to a curious ring of eyes watching her. A whole tribe of runaway children—black, white, and Mexican—had already staked out a communal shelter there. Their leader was a young man not much older than Maya. They asked her name, where she was from, and why she was there.

Her truthful answers satisfied them, and she was welcomed into the group and told the rules: they didn't steal because it might bring the police, and they didn't share cars for sleeping unless it rained (very few were watertight). They collected bottles for their return money; they took odd jobs around the community; they took their clothes to be washed at a laundromat; and on Friday nights when one of the group's family was at work, they took baths at his house and did their ironing. They also vied for prizes at weekly jitterbug dance contests, and here Maya made her contribution. She and a Mexican boy won a second prize of $10.

They were on their own, but they worked together to survive and the color of their skins or their family histories or their educations were of no consequence. Living from hand to mouth in the junkyard gave Maya a sense of self-confidence she had never known before.

She lived with her new friends for a month. Then she called Vivian and asked for fare home to San Francisco. Vivian said she would send a ticket to Bailey, Sr. Without explanation, Maya suggested it might be easier simply to deal with a travel agent. Vivian asked no questions and arranged the return trip. Not wanting to say good-bye to her vagabond friends, Maya spent the night before her departure in an all-night movie.

From this experience Maya gained an abiding knowledge of herself, of her own resources, and a strong tolerance for other people's differences. Her small community of homeless friends had accepted one another without question. "After a month my thinking processes had changed that I hardly recognized myself," she writes.

During World War II women became conductors on the cable cars for the first time.

Back at her mother's house in San Francisco, Maya was upset to see that Bailey and Vivian were locked in a struggle that could have no happy resolution. Bailey, at sixteen, was trying to compete for Vivian's attention by imitating the sophisticated men who hung around her. Vivian still wanted her son to be a boy and take orders from her. One night after Bailey missed getting home on time, his mother threw him out. And to Maya's astonishment, he went.

Bailey's leaving left Maya restless. "The need for change bulldozed a road down the center of my mind," she recalls. She wasn't ready to go back to school. She told Vivian she wanted to get a job. Her mother didn't object, but she wanted to know what Maya had in mind. Maya knew she needed a birth certificate to prove her age at the shipyards or defense plants. She didn't want to be a secretary (she had chosen not to take typing in school because it wasn't intellectual enough), and she wasn't quite sure what else was possible.

She had noticed, however, that women had begun to replace men as conductors on the streetcars in San Francisco. With so many men called into the armed services during the war, many traditionally male jobs were opened up to women. She decided that she wanted to be a conductor on a cable car. "They don't accept colored people on the streetcars," Vivian told her.

Maya brooded about that for a while. Then her determination started to grow. She told her mother she was going to try for the job regardless. Vivian replied immediately, "Give it everything you've got. I've told you many times, 'Can't do is like don't care.' Neither of them have a home here."

Maya began her siege of the Market Street Railroad Company. She arrived every morning promptly at nine and made her application through the same receptionist, who kept telling her that they only hired through agencies or that there were no openings. Maya would then show the woman ads that had been placed in the paper and would ask for the name of the personnel director. When told he was busy, Maya would say she would wait. She often waited all day. The civil rights groups to whom she took her case thought she was crazy. There were job openings at higher pay all over the city. They, of course, didn't know that she was underage.

Vivian fixed her daughter breakfast every morning and gave her carfare and lunch money. She never required a progress report. And Maya never gave her any details of the day before. Vivian occasionally would remind her daughter that "God helps those who help themselves," but gave no direct advice.

It took four weeks for Maya to break down the defenses of the streetcar company. She finally became the first woman and the first black conductor on the cable cars. She was given the worst schedule in the system. The company may have hoped it would discourage her. She was assigned the earliest and the latest shifts, but Vivian arranged her own schedule so she could drive Maya out to the car barn at 4:30 in the morning or pick her up from a night's work at 2 A.M. Vivian never complained. Looking back, Maya writes that this period marked the beginning of a mutual respect that she and her mother would spend a lifetime developing between them.

In the spring of 1944, Maya returned to school. It held little interest for her after living in the junkyard on her own and running a cable car. "Without willing it," she writes in *I Know Why the Caged Bird Sings*, "I had gone from being ignorant of being ignorant to being aware of being aware.... I knew that I knew very little, but I was certain that the things I had yet to learn wouldn't be taught me at George Washington High School."

She started cutting classes until Vivian confronted her about it. Her mother's message was simple: If Maya didn't want to go to school, all she had to do was tell her mother, and they could work something out. But what Vivian couldn't forgive was Maya putting her in the position of having a white school official call her up and tell her something about her daughter that she didn't already know. Maya respected that and stopped cutting classes. But it didn't make her feel any better about being trapped in a white school.

Once Maya returned to school, Vivian returned to her many business enterprises, which included setting up nightclubs to entertain all the servicemen in San Francisco. Left on her own, Maya continued to try to satisfy her enormous appetite for reading. She explored, through books, the emotions and passions her adolescent body was becoming responsive to. She read about lesbians, women who are sexually attracted to other women, with great compassion. She began to wonder if, in fact, she might be a lesbian herself. Vivian assured her she was not, but Maya still had questions about why she was so tall and flat-chested when she was almost sixteen.

Not knowing quite how to test her sexual preference, she propositioned a young man from the neighborhood, whom she rather liked. He was surprised but accommodating.

Maya was very disappointed. The event, which in the many books she read was accompanied by wild, poetry-inspiring sensations, had been impersonal in real life. She dismissed it in confusion, figuring it would make more sense in time. In less than a month she realized that she was pregnant.

A teenage Maya Angelou posed for a publicity shot in the early 1940s.

CHAPTER 4

PICK 'EM UP AND LAY 'EM DOWN

*I hadn't time to be a poet, I had to find a job, get my
grits together, and take care of my son.*
—Maya Angelou

Maya carried around her secret for several
months, not knowing quite what to do. With a characteristic honesty that would later distinguish her writing, she faced up to the fact that she had no one to
blame but herself for what had happened. The young
man she had so blatantly challenged to make love to
her could not be held responsible for making her
pregnant.

"For eons, it seemed, I had accepted my plight as the
hapless, put-upon victim of fate and the Furies, but this
time I had to face the fact that I had brought my new
catastrophe upon myself," she writes "… so I hefted
the burden of pregnancy at sixteen onto my own
shoulders where it belonged."

She wrote to her brother, who was now in the merchant marines. He advised against telling Vivian on the grounds that she might make Maya quit school. Bailey said school would be impossible after the baby came, so Maya should stick out her last year and get a diploma.

Maya went along with Bailey's advice, partly, she later wrote, because she hadn't thought too much about the baby or what taking care of a baby would mean. She was only sixteen years old and motherhood was not something she and her classmates discussed.

Whether it was the subconscious knowledge that her life would be radically changed in a few months or whether she just redirected her energies, Maya began to apply herself vigorously to her schoolwork again. Seeing that, Vivian assumed her daughter was all right. She busied herself with her own enterprises and didn't notice the physical changes in Maya's body. She began to look rather buxom, which she liked, and the family must have assumed this was part of an adolescent girl's natural development.

Besides, there were other things on people's minds. The war in Europe was declared over on May 8, V-E Day, which celebrated the victory in Europe for the United States and its Allies over Hitler and the Germans. Attention was now shifted to ending the war with the Japanese in the Pacific.

So Maya played the part of the committed student and no one questioned her. When the spring term ended, she happily applied for the summer session. She completed her requirements in time to graduate in August. "I burrowed myself into caves of facts and found delight in the logical resolutions of mathematics," she later wrote.

On August 6 and August 9, 1945, atomic bombs were dropped on Hiroshima and Nagasaki, bringing the war with Japan to a close. Maya graduated from high school less than a week later and dropped her bomb on the family. She left a note on her stepfather's pillow that said, "I am sorry to bring this disgrace upon the family, but I am pregnant."

For the next three weeks Maya was taken to doctors and to department stores in preparation for the baby's birth. Her son, Clyde, was born on time with no complications, and he was brought home to a house well stocked with diapers and baby wraps.

Maya thought he was beautiful but fragile. Vivian handled the infant with an almost casual confidence that her daughter simply couldn't emulate. Maya was afraid of hurting the child. He was so helpless, she felt completely unprepared to meet his needs. Finally, Vivian put Clyde in bed with his mother one night over Maya's protests. She was scared she might roll over and crush him in her sleep. She tried to stay awake and watch over him but drifted off in spite of herself. When Vivian woke Maya several hours later, the new mother found that she, even in her sleep, was carefully shielding the infant by instinct. She was a real mother after all.

Vivian and Daddy Clidell offered to take care of the baby while Maya continued her education. As a single parent at seventeen, armed only with a high school diploma, she chose instead to try to make her way— with her son—in the world. Her reasons were not clear to her at the time, but in retrospect she saw that several factors were at work.

She sensed the breaking down of her mother and Daddy Clidell's marriage. And she knew that Vivian was worried about money. With the war over, the flush days for blacks in the city were coming to an end, and Vivian lived off those cash-rich big spenders. Even her boarders were having to move back home

Black soldiers served in a segregated army for the duration of
World War II.

because their jobs were dependent on entertainment-
starved servicemen. The black servicemen were being
discharged fast and steady work wasn't easy to find.

Blacks who thought that the integration of the armed
forces would bring brotherhood to the peacetime
workplace were mistaken. Defense plants closed and
let their employees go. The new unemployed had to
compete with discharged servicemen—heroes home
from the front—for what jobs were available. Women,

too, who had worked shoulder to shoulder with men in wartime factories and shipyards, were now having trouble getting jobs that paid decently. Blacks were at the bottom of the job pool.

Maya didn't want to be a burden to her mother. As generous and kind as her mother was, Maya knew there were limits. She also remembered ruefully how she and Bailey had been shipped to their grandmother without explanation. She had no reason to believe that Vivian would treat Clyde any better, and she didn't want to ever make Clyde feel as abandoned as she had felt as a child.

With the birth of her son, Maya began the long struggle to try to control her own life. She would fall prey to her worst weaknesses—her fantasies and unrealistic expectations, but through it all she would keep her true self intact somehow. Her creativity during the next ten years would be directed toward survival for herself and her son. These would be the years of gathering experience and of finding out who she was.

Maya's first efforts at getting a white-collar job were hopeless. The telephone company tried to tell her she had failed a simple test. She didn't have the heart to fight it because she was desperate to start paying her own way. She finally ended up convincing the owner of a fast-food restaurant that she was an experienced Creole cook. She enlisted one of her mother's boarders to help her fill that gap in her cooking education. He assured her that garlic, green peppers, and tomatoes could turn any dish into Creole cooking.

Maya found a room for Clyde and herself and a woman to look after the baby while she was at work. The restaurant owner was happy with her pseudo-Creole cooking. Like the meat in the stew pots that absorbed her spices, she soaked up the rich life that flowed in and out of the cafe. She writes that "near the steam counter, the soft sounds of black talk, the sharp reports of laughter, and the shuffling feet on tiled floors mixed themselves in odorous vapors...." She was content.

Her happiness was completely fulfilled when she met Charles, a man she describes "as perfection." He was everything she dreamed a boyfriend would be: handsome, gentle, fond of Clyde, and fun to talk to. Of course he also had a fiancée he was waiting for (she was finishing up a job at a defense plant) before returning to Louisiana. He told Maya this, but she was too smitten to pay attention. She spent all her extra cash buying him presents and dreaming of their perfect future together. Their room would be pink and Clyde's would be yellow, and she would cook just for them in a perfect kitchen. She even saw herself planting roses by their picket fence.

When he left, as he had said he would, Maya was devastated. Her fantasizing and her impulsiveness would mature into a vivid imagination and the strength to take both personal and artistic risks. But for now, at the age of eighteen, she writes that she was "like a tree or river that merely responded to the winds and the tides."

Bailey, who was on leave from the merchant marines, got worried about her depression but had very little sympathy for her self-pity. He told her, "If you want to stay around here looking like death eating a soda cracker, that's your business." He encouraged her to pick up and move to a different city and start over. Maya decided that was a good idea.

She set out for Los Angeles where there were some Baxter relatives, whom she assumed she could stay with until she got settled. She called them from the railroad station on her arrival, and they came to pick her up. After an hour's visit, they asked when she needed to catch her train connection. Humiliated, Maya returned to the railroad station and bought a ticket for San Diego. More than twenty-five years later, when Maya Angelou was to write about this period in her young life in *Gather Together in My Name*, she admitted that she had not really known what she was doing. "What passed for mind was animal instinct," she writes.

Lonely, but proud, she followed her heart instead of her head into one misadventure after another. Maya had a gift for finding good women to take care of Clyde while she worked. And the women she found usually ended up looking after Maya, too. Her devotion to the child was real and they responded to that. Mother Cleo in San Diego was typical. She reminded Maya of her Grandmother Henderson. Mother Cleo took Maya into her house, as well as Clyde, so the two would have more time together.

Clyde's life was secure now, but Maya's life away from him and Mother Cleo's healthy home took a turn for the worse. She got a job as a cocktail waitress in a local nightclub and eventually became entangled in the prostitution business.

For a few months, Maya straddled two different worlds. In the one, she was a madam for prostitutes, living outside the law, wheeling and dealing with people in the underworld—a world of deception, greed, and lust. In the other, she was a hard-working, church-going, devoted, and responsible mother. Within this world she also had an intellectual and artistic life. She took modern dance lessons, and she read.

In her reading she discovered the nineteenth-century Russian writers Dostoevski, Chekhov, Gorky, and Turgenev. Their vision of life fit hers perfectly. She writes, "I walked the sunny California streets shrouded in Russian mists...." These writers explore the darker, more complex side of human nature—a side Maya was experiencing every day.

Dostoevski's novel *Crime and Punishment* struck her with particular force. The novel is about a man who murders an old woman and her sister and steals their money. He then tries to rationalize the act by arguing that he will do good things with the money. Maya justified her actions in the same way. Like the Dostoevski character, Maya finally realized that morally there could be no justification for what she was doing.

Mother Cleo's generosity and trust made Maya ashamed of how she was living. She was not comfortable deceiving someone who had been good to her and her child. She also was afraid that if she were arrested, the courts would declare her an unfit mother and take Clyde away from her. Her fears were unbearable, so she packed up Clyde late one night, drove to the railroad station, and slipped out of town by train. She headed straight for Stamps.

Two realities greeted Maya's homecoming– her grandmother's world, where sternness was mixed with love, and the hateful racist world of a small southern town. Although she had been discriminated against in San Francisco, Maya had not directly felt the sharp shards of southern racism there. Now they pierced her mind and soul.

One day, while shopping in the white part of Stamps, she was insulted by a saleswoman in a white store. Maya told the woman off in no uncertain terms, feeling very proud of herself for standing up for her rights. She raced home to tell Momma. When she began to regale her grandmother with the story of her triumph, she was met with a stony silence and a slap in the face. Momma had already received a phone call about the incident.

Maya writes that her grandmother lashed out at her. "You think 'cause you been to California, these crazy people won't kill you? You think those lunatic cracker boys won't try to catch you in the road and violate you? You think because of your all-fire principle some of the men won't feel like putting their white sheets on and riding over here to stir up trouble? You do and you're wrong. Ain't nothing to protect you and us but the good Lord and some miles." Momma had already packed Maya and the baby's things and arranged for a member of the church to drive them in a horse and buggy to the nearest safe railroad depot.

Nineteen-year-old Maya returned to her mother's house in San Francisco and contemplated the future. She decided she would join the army to get some serious vocational training and let Vivian—in spite of all Maya's reservations—take care of the baby.

In an odd twist of fate, the drama and dance lessons she had taken in high school prevented Maya from joining the army. Evidently the school was on a government list of suspected communist organizations. In the days right after World War II, the Cold War broke out, a period of tension and open hostility between the USSR and the Western democracies. Some Americans, afraid of communist subversion within the country, used some very undemocratic methods to search out people they believed to be disloyal. In Maya's case, the army accused her of being a communist because she took dance and drama lessons at the California Labor School when she was fourteen. The officials, who had originally accepted Maya's application for the army, turned her down when they did a security check.

Maya's plans to bring her life into focus were shattered. She found a job as a short-order cook and again drifted through the days. Although unknown to her at the time, her rejection by the army was a blessing. Her creative inner life was about to take shape.

Music and dance had always been a part of her life, from the gospels she sang at the Christian Methodist Episcopal Church in Stamps to her mother teaching her the Time Step in St. Louis. In high school, she had even gone as far as seriously studying modern ballet and dance theory at the California Labor School. Her attendance at this school may have blocked her entrance into the armed forces, but it was now going to lift her into show business.

One of Maya's pleasures during this time was hanging out at a record store nearby. In the late 1940s, record stores had sound booths where customers could listen to new records before they decided to buy them. The owner of the store introduced Maya to the jazz of Charlie "Bird" Parker, Max Roach, Dizzy Gillespie, Bud Powell, and Al Haig. Maya loved all the black performers, from the singers of spirituals and gospel to the calypso rhythms of the West Indies that told wonderful, funny stories.

The owner of the record store liked Maya and so when a man came around looking for a dancer, she gave him Maya's address. When R.L. Poole knocked on Maya's door and asked if she were "Rita" Johnson, the dancer, she confessed that she was. R.L. was looking for a new tap dance partner for his nightclub act.

After an embarrassing audition R.L. hired Maya, and she began her new life. "I committed myself to a show business career, and dancing and studying dance."

Bailey's life also took a turn for the better. His marriage to a young woman named Eunice brought him back from the cynicism he had developed after leaving home and finding the world unreceptive to bright, young black men. Eunice restored his sense of humor.

The music of jazz musicians Charlie "Bird" Parker (center) and Miles Davis (right) had a positive influence on young Maya Angelou.

He was optimistic and full of fun again, and Maya was grateful.

"Poole and Rita" made their debut performance. Maya was so excited she froze in front of the audience. But R.L. forgave her and she began to relish their appearances. She gave up her job as a short-order cook to spend more time rehearsing with R.L. She was convinced that she and R.L. were on their way to the big time. She worked hard at dancing and began to see herself as an artist. Looking back much later, she saw that she loved the discipline of dancing and the thrill of performing. "I was a hungry person invited to a welcome table for the first time in her life," Maya writes of her break into show business.

Then R.L.'s former partner, a dimpled, pretty heroin addict, showed up to claim her old job back. R.L. didn't even put up a fight. Maya was on her own again.

Vivian told her about a cooking job in Stockton. Maya thought a new start in another town was just what she needed. She found a motherly Indian women called Big Mary to take care of Clyde during the week, and she took a room elsewhere for herself. She was very lonely and spent her free time either shopping for new clothes she had no place to wear or reading. For once, even reading didn't absorb her full attention.

In the midst of this unsatisfying life, tragedy struck. One day when she was on her way to see Clyde, the landlord caught up with her at the door. There were frantic messages from San Francisco. Vivian and Eunice, Bailey's new wife, were in the hospital and Maya was needed immediately. She ran to Clyde's babysitter and explained that she had to go home on a family emergency, hugged the baby, and raced to the bus station.

Although Vivian had come through an operation without any problems, Maya discovered Bailey collapsed in his mother's hospital room. His beloved Eunice had died of pneumonia and tuberculosis that morning.

Bailey cried and talked through the night. He finally slept for a few hours. He awoke a closed shell. After the funeral, he told Maya he never wanted to hear Eunice's name again. Maya recognized even then that she was losing a part of Bailey forever as he sealed off the pain. Within a few days, he quit his job with the railroad and started hanging out with old street friends.

Heartbroken, Maya returned to Stockton and walked into a mother's worst nightmare. Big Mary's house was boarded up when Maya arrived. There was no sign that she or Clyde had ever been there.

Maya Angelou went to Israel in 1955 with the cast of *Porgy and Bess.*

CHAPTER 5

WALKING ON THE EDGE

Music was my refuge. I could crawl into the spaces between notes and curl my back to loneliness.
—Maya Angelou

A neighbor called to Maya. "You looking for your baby?" she asked. Maya nodded and the neighbor announced that Big Mary, the babysitter, had moved out three days before with no forwarding address. In fact, she had told the neighbor that Maya had given Clyde to her because she didn't have time to take care of him.

The neighbor said she was pretty sure that the baby-sitter had a brother in Bakersfield, California. Maya boarded a bus to Bakersfield and appealed to black cab drivers at the station to help her in her quest. It wasn't easy to locate a man whose name and face she didn't know, but her determination mobilized her wits. She talked one of the cab drivers into helping her. Maya knew that Big Mary didn't drink often, but when she did, she did it in a big way. Maya and the cab driver began a search of all the black bars in Bakersfield. She finally found a bartender who could give them a name and address, and she found Clyde playing in the mud in front of Big Mary's brother's house. The boy was as glad to see her as she was to see him.

Maya and Clyde returned to San Francisco, and Maya started job hunting again. She landed a job in a restaurant in Oakland that catered to the boxing crowd. Troubadour Martin, a tall, quiet, black man on the fringes of the boxing world, offered her a job selling dresses out of her room. It meant Maya could spend her days with Clyde and still support herself, so she never asked if the dresses were stolen; she simply agreed to do it.

Troub treated Maya so kindly and respectfully that she began to put him into her fantasies of a husband and protector. She knew that he had a heroin habit, but she figured if she could share that with him, they might make a life together. When she asked him about it, he just shrugged her off. But Maya was persistent, and finally, he took her to the San Francisco waterfront to a rundown hotel. It was filled with addicts, and their writhing bodies were draped around every room. Troub took her to the bathroom where he slowly, ritualistically shot up with heroin. Maya was revolted; she begged him to stop. He made her watch the whole process. Then he asked if she wanted any. In tears now, she said no.

"Then promise me you won't ever use it," he said. "Promise me you'll stay nice like I found you." Maya promised. And she understood that he had exposed himself to her in all the weakness of his addiction to save her. It was a generous and loving gesture, and she appreciated it.

She returned to her apartment the next day. It took two shifts of short-order cooking to pay for a room and a sitter for Clyde. Although Maya was relieved to have work, she felt her life was going nowhere. She did, however, manage to hold on to the things that fed her creatively. When she could, she would spend the two hours between jobs listening to new records at a nearby record store, read at the library, or sometimes take a dance class at the YWCA.

When the white owner of the record store offered her a job, she almost didn't take it. She was still suspicious of white people and was afraid of being exploited. But the money would enable her to move back in with Vivian and see more of Clyde, so she took the job.

The months she spent working at the record store were blessed. "For two years," she writes, she and Clyde "had spun like water spiders in a relentless eddy." Now, "life shimmered with beautiful colors." Once again she could live a normal life with her son, and on top of this she could listen to the wealth of music that surrounded her every day. Her suspicion of Louise Cox, the owner of the store who had hired her, also finally melted away, and for the first time Maya had a friendly relationship with a white person.

While working in the record store, Maya met Tosh Angeles, a Greek-American man, who was interested in good black jazz. Tosh was handsome and quiet and took a real interest in Clyde, taking him on outings and teaching him to play ball. Maya took him home, where Vivian gave him a cool reception. Not only was he white but he was poor, and the combination was untenable. Bailey, on the other hand, thought if Maya loved the man, she ought to do what she wanted to do.

Maya married Tosh without the benefit of her mother's blessing. Vivian moved to Los Angeles a week before the event. Maya gave up her job and settled down to being what she thought was a typical housewife. And Tosh was a storybook husband. She cooked and cleaned and was ecstatically happy for almost a year, giving in to small things because the marriage itself was so important. Tosh didn't like most of her friends, but he encouraged her to continue her dance lessons, and he was very good to Clyde.

Maya was not aware at first of how much of herself she was crushing in an effort to have a perfect marriage. It was her husband's telling Clyde that there was no God that unleashed all her stifled instincts. Her grandmother's God was as real to her as her grandmother, she discovered. The more Tosh argued against the concept of God, the more she felt compelled to go to church behind his back.

Tosh was cutting at Maya's roots, roots she had not really acknowledged before as an adult. The conflict was tearing her apart spiritually. Then she came down with appendicitis, which caused serious blood poisoning. Coming back to consciousness in the hospital, Maya begged Tosh to send her to Arkansas to recuperate. She knew that she could get well if she could be near Momma again. Poor Tosh. He had to tell her that while she was being operated on, they had received word of Momma's death.

The marriage never recovered. Maya recognized that she could not cut herself off from her background or the spirituality of her religion. She was also mature enough to know that it was not Tosh's fault that he couldn't make all her dreams of a perfect marriage come true.

Tosh left some money in their bank account. Maya stayed home for a while and tried to reassure Clyde, who loved Tosh, that she was not going to stop loving her son. When the money ran out, she set out to find another job. She was twenty-two years old and was tired of cooking in restaurants. She wanted to use her creative talents to make a living.

Maya worked briefly at a local nightclub, which was little more than a sleazy strip bar. Unlike the other dancers, who moved languidly to slow music, hoping to be sexually enticing, Maya was interested only in showing how she could really dance. She choreographed her dances in a free-wheeling combination of jitterbug, jazz, and modern dance. She was determined not to lose her toe-hold on show business.

Part of her job was to push drinks on the customers to supplement her salary. She got a quarter for every champagne cocktail she got a customer to buy her (it was really ginger ale) and $2 for each $8 bottle of champagne. But Maya wanted to dance, not sell drinks. So the first week she didn't. The manager of the club threatened to fire her if she didn't come back after her number and sit with the customers.

Well, she decided to herself, she would sit with the customers, but she would explain the drink situation to them and let them choose what to do. And she would come out in street clothes, not in a robe over her costume. Having satisfied her own moral code, she became almost sassy with the customers.

The audience found everything about her refreshing; they came back, and they spread the word about this new dancing phenomenon at the strip joint who told you your drinks were really soda and that you get a better deal with the bottles of champagne and what her cut was. Instead of tired, lonely men, the usual audience at these kinds of nightclubs, she started attracting middle-class couples and curious show business people from San Francisco's cabarets.

Cabarets were very popular in the 1950s. These tiny clubs usually featured singers or comedians on small stages. The audiences enjoyed the sophisticated music and topical humor in an intimate setting. San Francisco had several successful cabarets that launched the careers of a number of top performers. The comedian Mort Sahl got his start at the Hungry I, for example. Scouts from New York and Chicago learned to check out the San Francisco cabarets regularly for new talent.

The owners of the Purple Onion, a popular San Francisco cabaret, came to see Maya one night. They came back a second time with their current attraction, a singer who called herself Jorie. She invited Maya to a private party after the show.

Maya felt out of place among the cabaret crowd at the party and became a little defensive. When Jorie made disparaging remarks about calypso music, Maya felt obliged to defend this West Indian form of folk singing by performing a number without accompaniment. The people at the party went wild. Maya, who considered herself neither a singer nor an expert on calypso, had sung the song just to defend herself and all black people against a slur. To her enormous surprise, she was offered a job at the Purple Onion singing calypso. She was to replace Jorie, who was going to New York.

Her friends were as astonished as she was. She had never sung anywhere but in church. She had no musical arrangements and her repertoire of calypso songs was very limited. But Maya saw the offer, improbable as it was, as an opportunity to enter a world of exciting people and to use her creative powers to make a decent living for herself and her son. She had taught herself the Time Step to please Vivian. Now she would teach herself calypso to please the managers of the Purple Onion.

The managers of the Purple Onion seemed more concerned about her name than her singing abilities. Maya then called herself Rita Johnson in public (Maya

The Purple Onion is where Marguerite Johnson first used the stage name Maya Angelou.

was used only within the family). The Purple Onion staff felt the name was not catchy enough for a performer. She told them about "Maya," and they loved it. But Maya Johnson didn't work either. She told them her married name was Angeles, and it didn't take long to adapt that to Angelou. Marguerite Johnson became Maya Angelou when she debuted at the Purple Onion.

Jorie had introduced Maya to her dramatic coach, Lloyd Clark. He hid whatever reservations he had about Maya's inexperience and began working with her on an act. She already knew how to move as a dancer. He taught her how to stand still and hold an audience. The piano player at the Purple Onion was stunned when he realized that Maya didn't read music or know what key she sang in, but her honesty and appeals for help won him over. He helped her arrange the calypso songs she knew from a few records into her own dramatic renditions. She was grateful for all the coaching and she worked hard. She knew her musical limitations—she didn't have perfect pitch—and she learned to compensate with humor, talking intimately to the audience, and doing some dance steps.

Maya was an instant hit and quickly became a celebrity in San Francisco. There was an honesty to her style. If she forgot the words to a song, she admitted it and improvised. She built a rapport with the audience that was warm and immediate.

Suddenly Maya had a contract, good money, and a following. She was interviewed by the press and asked to sing on the radio. She became a sought-after guest for parties among a wider group in San Francisco than the cabaret crowd. She met writers and painters and patrons of the arts, people who had read as much as she had and wanted to talk about books and ideas. Because she conveyed in her act an interesting personality, other people wanted to know her opinion on subjects much broader than calypso music.

The experience of working at the Purple Onion was to usher Maya into a world that even her fertile imagination had not prepared her for. It was as if her whole life had been flowing toward this narrow opening where she would emerge into the vast expanses of art and creativity. From this point forward Maya's creative life would also be her working life.

Maya had crossed a line. She had become a respected artist in the community of artists. Among the artists Maya met was a Greek painter, Varda Yanko. Through Yanko, Maya says, she entered "a world strange and fanciful." She met other performers, artists, and political activists from all over the world.

With this exposure, she began to question, as she puts it, her own "tribal myths" about whites.

She tells of one particular incident at one of Yanko's parties. During the party, Maya became engrossed in a debate with a group of people about a recent Supreme Court decision that would desegregate schools. Two of the people arguing with Maya were a black man and a blonde-haired woman. When Maya learned that the white woman was the black man's wife, she moved away from the couple psychologically.

She firmly believed the general caution that was given in her community that a white woman would just use a black man and then desert him. But after the party, when she examined this idea, she realized there was little that a white woman could take a black man for—certainly not his money—and she concluded that "the logic of the warning did not hold."

When the popular Broadway show *New Faces of 1953* came to San Francisco, the whole cast came to see Maya. She was offered a part in the show but had to turn it down because of her Purple Onion contract. Despite the disappointment, she felt that she had proven something to herself—that she had imagination and talent.

Another import from Broadway completely be-dazzled Maya. It was an all-black production of George Gershwin's opera *Porgy and Bess*, starring Leontyne Price, William Warfield, and Cab Calloway, among others. Maya writes about how she was trans-fixed by one of the dancers:

> The dancer moved out her reach, flinging her legs high, carrying the music in her body as if it were a private thing, given into her care and protection....I wanted to be with her on the stage letting the music fly through my body. Her torso seemed to lose solidity and float, defying gravity....I wanted to be her.

In 1952, the cast of *Porgy and Bess* left for an extended tour of Europe. From left to right, Levern Hutcherson, Urylee Leonardos, Leontyne Price, William Warfield and Cab Calloway who portrayed Sportin' Life.

She hadn't known the musical theater could be so powerful. She had never seen an opera before and had seen very few musicals.

Success uncorked all the creative energy she had been storing up during her twenty-five years of coping with life as it came to her. She started digging into her own poetry, often written during difficult times in her life, and adapting it to calypso rhythms. More and more she added her own material to her act.

Maya had never aspired to be a singer—it just happened to her. At the Purple Onion, it was more her presentation than her singing voice that drew in the patrons. This became painfully clear when she met Fred Wilkerson, or Wilkie as he was called. Wilkie was a voice teacher, who she met through the cast of *Porgy and Bess*. He told her that her singing was "totally wrong." He also said that he could help her, but "only if you work hard and listen to me." The lessons would soon serve her well.

The cast and producers of *Porgy and Bess* came to see Maya at the Purple Onion. And, almost like a dream, she was asked to audition for the role played by the dancer that had so captivated her. The company was being sponsored by the U.S. State Department to do a European tour, and they needed a new dancer. To see Europe—all the fabled places she had read about in books—was the most exciting prospect Maya could imagine. But she also knew she couldn't get out of her contract at the Purple Onion for another three months and the tour would have started by then. She auditioned anyway to prove to herself that she had the talent. Maya got the part and then refused it.

When her contract ran out at the Purple Onion, Maya went to New York to audition for a Truman Capote play on Broadway. It was a chance for her to become a nationally known performer. The day she got that role, she also got a telegram from the producers of *Porgy and Bess*. The show was in Canada, ready to leave for Europe. Did she still want the part?

"Even my imagination had never dared to include me in Europe," writes Maya. None of the images in movies, books, or newsreels had "included a six-foot-tall black woman hovering either in the back or in the foreground."

Only one thing held her back: leaving Clyde for a year, which was the length of the tour. How could she justify to herself abandoning him like that? Vivian was back in San Francisco and promised to take good care of him, but Maya knew that wasn't the same as having his mother with him. If she went to New York, Clyde would come with her. She struggled with her dilemma. In the end, she decided to go with *Porgy and Bess*.

Europe overwhelmed Maya. The literature she had read throughout her life poured over her. In Verona, Italy, she walked through streets that were the setting for Shakespeare's *Romeo and Juliet*. She was incredulous that fate had brought her "into the bright sun of Italy, into a town made famous by one of the world's greatest writers." This amazement was not shared by the other more worldly and jaded members of the troupe. After a few sarcastic comments about her naive enthusiasm, Maya kept her wonderment to herself.

Maya performed in all the famous opera houses from Paris to Cairo. And in each new place she used her well-developed ear (and a grammar book) to learn the native language and talk with the people.

The black touring company's acceptance by the people in every country *Porgy and Bess* played in was astounding to Maya. Crowds mobbed the troupe after their performances; men flung themselves at Maya and the other female members of the company. Maya saw this as the twisted logic of racism in the United States. The very country that denied blacks equality at home had provided these artists with the official sanction that made them sought after abroad.

The tour of Europe and parts of Northern Africa was exhilarating for Maya, but there was never a moment she did not think of her son. She was awash in guilt. She writes that "the black mother perceives destruction at every door, ruination at each window, and even she herself is not beyond her own suspicion." She left the company before the tour ended.

When she arrived back in San Francisco, she found that her fears were well-founded. Clyde had a terrible rash that doctors could not cure. Only Maya's presence could heal her son. Swallowing her guilt, she set out to repair the damage done to Clyde's body and emotions.

In 1957, Maya was featured in Columbia Pictures *Calypso Heat Wave*.

CHAPTER 6

STILL I'LL RISE

You may encounter many defeats, but you must not be defeated.
— Vivian Baxter
(Maya's mother)

As a mother, Maya had learned from the *Porgy and Bess* tour that she could not afford such long separations from her son. Remembering the hurt of separation in her own childhood made her all the more determined not to inflict that kind of pain on Clyde again. She would spend the next four years touring the West Coast and Hawaii with her cabaret act, taking Clyde with her.

During this time, Maya's relationship with her son was to take on a different shape as he grew into being his own person. In the third volume of her autobiography, she describes Clyde's transformation:

> Before my eyes a physical and mental metamorphosis began
> as gradually and inexorably as a seasonal change…. I noticed
> that he no longer rushed panting to my room to assure
> himself that I was still there. And when I left the house to
> shop we both took the parting normally, with a casual "See
> you in a minute." His shoulders began to ride high again and
> he had opinions about everything from the planning of the
> meals to what he wanted to be called.

What Clyde wanted to be called was "Guy." He informed his mother that he was intent on changing his name. He even refused to respond to his old name. After months of training his family, "Guy" finally stuck for good.

While Maya and Guy were pulling their personal lives back together, the lives of black Americans were undergoing profound changes. It was the late 1950s. The times were a strange mixture of things changing and things staying the same. Racism was still alive and well, but black people were rising up and fighting back as never before. In 1955, blacks in Montgomery, Alabama, used their economic power as a weapon against racism. They began a boycott of the city buses that would bring the bus company near bankruptcy and work a financial hardship on the city's merchants.

In Maya's home state of Arkansas, the governor called out the National Guard to prevent nine black children from attending an all-white high school in Little Rock. President Eisenhower responded by ordering the U.S. Army into Little Rock to escort the children into the school and protect them. Maya sensed that the country was moving in some direction, but as she writes, "no one knew our destination nor our arrival date."

Like the budding civil rights movement, Maya was struggling to define herself. She was creating all the material for her nightclub acts and had written and recorded six songs for Liberty Records. But she began

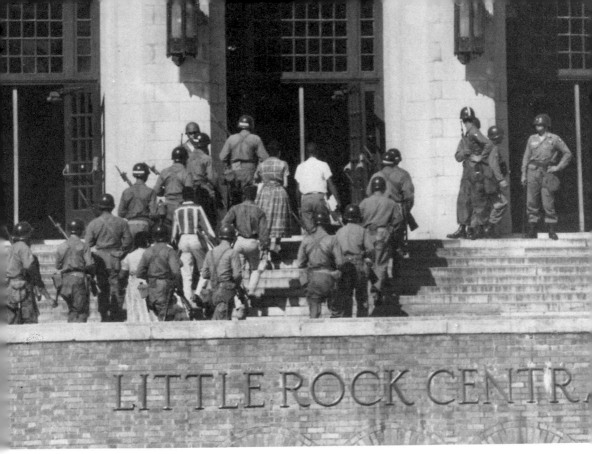

U.S. soldiers helped the forced integration of schools in Maya's home state of Arkansas in September, 1957.

to see her work as superficial and trivial, "singing clever little songs only moderately well," as she puts it. Blacks all around her were doing serious work. Lorraine Hansberry had written an important, unsentimental play about the black American family. The play, *Raisin in the Sun*, was being performed on Broadway in New York City. James Baldwin blasted away white myths about blacks in his book *The Fire Next Time*, as did John Killens in his book *And Then We Heard Thunder*, which was about black soldiers in a white army.

These writers' accomplishments pushed Maya to attempt other forms of writing—character sketches, short stories, plays. Writing was a natural creative direction for Maya to go in. Rich language forms had

James Baldwin, author of *Native Son*.

flowed constantly through her life. It had comforted her and given her inspiration. She had written poetry since she was a child, but more as a way to ease the pain of growing up and to understand herself and the world. This was not enough now. She needed to move beyond this, to take herself seriously as a writer. "If I ended in defeat," she writes of her decision, "at least I would be trying. Trying to overcome was black people's honorable tradition."

While working in Los Angeles she made friends with John Killens, who was in Hollywood to write the screenplay for his book, *Youngblood*. She asked Killens to read some of her work-in-progress. He told her that her writing needed polishing but that she had an undeniable talent. He suggested she come to New York and work with the Harlem Writers Guild, an informal group of black writers who met regularly to hear and criticize each other's works. Maya took courage.

When Guy was fourteen, she decided to take Killens's advice about moving to New York. John and his wife, Grace, lived in Brooklyn with their two children, who were close to Guy's age. They helped Maya get settled in their neighborhood.

Maya's first reading at the Harlem Writers Guild took place at the Killens's house. She offered the gathering the first act of a play she had titled *One Life, One Love*. No performance in a theater had ever given her such stage fright. Maya's description in her autobiography, *The Heart of a Woman*, is an agonizing picture of her first reading:

> I read the character and set description despite the sudden perversity of my body. The blood pounded in my ears but not enough to drown the skinny sound of my voice. My hands shook so that I had to lay the pages in my lap, but that was not a good solution due to the tricks my knees were playing. They lifted voluntarily, pulling my heels off the floor and then trembled like disturbed jello. Before I launched into the play's action, I looked around at the writers expecting but hoping not to see their amusement at my predicament. Their faces were studiously blank....
>
> Time wrapped itself around every word, slowing me. I couldn't force myself to read faster. The pages seemed to be multiplying even as I was trying to reduce them. The play was dull, the characters, unreal, and the dialogue was taken entirely off the back of a Campbell's soup can. I knew this was my first and last time at the Guild.

Members took notes throughout her reading. At the end, there was complete silence. John Henrik Clarke,

A Raisin in the Sun, by Lorraine Hansberry, was the first play by a black female to be produced on Broadway.

an editor and poet, finally said, "I found no life and very little love in the play from the opening of the act to its unfortunate end." Maya became paralyzed with humiliation.

Voices tittered. And other comments were thrown into the pot. Then Grace called people into the dining room for a drink. Killens came over to Maya. He thought she had got some very helpful insights from people and suggested she go into the other room so they wouldn't think she was too sensitive to take criticism next time. Maya decided not to say out loud what she was thinking about her host at that moment. She knew there wouldn't be any next time because they wouldn't have a writer as inept as she was waste their time again. She thought as she heard laughter in the other room, "They had stripped me, flayed me, utterly and completely undone me, and now they were as cheery as Christmas cards."

But later John Clarke, her worst critic, told her that he felt she had a story to tell and that he felt he could speak for the group in telling her they were glad to have her. Then he gave Maya the best advice a new writer can receive: "… in this group we remind each other that talent isn't enough. You've got to work. Write each sentence over and over again, until it seems you've used every combination possible, then write it again."

Paule Marshall, whose novel *Brown Girl, Brown Stones* was being made into a television movie, stopped Maya on the way out of the meeting. "You know, lots of people have more talent than you or I," she said conspiratorially. "Hard work makes the difference. Hard, hard, unrelenting work."

Maya thought about what she had learned that night. She decided that, because she read a lot and had a big vocabulary, she had taken words and the art of arranging them too lightly. "The writers assaulted my casual approach and made me confront my intention," she wrote in *The Heart of a Woman*. "If I wanted to write, I had to be willing to develop a kind of concentration found mostly in people awaiting execution. I had to learn technique and surrender my ignorance." Overall, she felt that the decision to be a writer "was a lot like deciding to jump into a frozen lake"—a shock but nevertheless exhilarating.

Struggling to learn the writer's art, Maya realized, was not going to pay the rent or feed a hungry teenage son. She booked herself into a club in New York's Greenwich Village for several weeks and decided that nothing could make her sing again after that engagement. It wasn't fresh or exciting anymore, and she wanted to do other things.

Her resolve to quit singing melted completely when she was offered a week's engagement at the legendary Apollo Theater in Harlem. During the Harlem Renaissance in the 1920s, the Apollo Theater made stars of many black musicians. Pearl Bailey, Dizzy Gillespie, Count Basie, and Duke Ellington had all played that stage on 125th Street.

The night she performed she brought the house down with an audience participation freedom song from Africa, a first for the Apollo, where audiences were supposed to be too sophisticated to want to sing along. During the performance and in the life around her, Maya sensed a change. Not just in Harlem, but among black people all over the country, she felt a stirring.

The leadership of the civil rights movement had fallen to a new young black minister in town, a recent Ph.D. named Martin Luther King, Jr. Dr. King and his Southern Christian Leadership Conference (SCLC) were beginning to mobilize southern blacks into non-

Dr. Martin Luther King, Jr. (center) and Ralph Abernathy (left)
were leaders of the nonviolent civil rights movement.

violent political action. When he came to New York to
raise money for the SCLC, Maya went to hear him with
Godfrey Cambridge, an actor friend of hers. They
listened raptly to Dr. King, who spoke in a church in
Harlem. He asked for help, and Maya and Godfrey sat
on a bench by the Hudson River afterwards to figure
out what to do. Between them they knew a lot of black
entertainers like themselves who were out of work.
Maya was sickened to see how many of the singers
from *Porgy and Bess*, for example, were unemployed.
Maybe, they thought, they could put on a play to raise
money for the cause. It would be about freedom, and

Maya would write it. Godfrey knew a good director and some first-rate performers who would be drawing cards.

Maya called the SCLC offices in New York and made an appointment to talk about their idea. She found the SCLC not only supportive but able to tap resources: they knew the owner of the Village Gate and negotiated free theater rental. It was an exciting and important undertaking not just for the SCLC and the cause, but also for black performers to showcase their talents. The idea, as wonderful as it was, created a crisis for Maya. SCLC officials wanted the subject matter to be appropriate, so they asked to see the script. Maya agreed, but of course she hadn't written anything yet. The project was taking off on the basis of a script that she found herself unable to write. She would sit down to an empty pad (she couldn't type) and nothing would come. "Mom," Guy would say, " you're trying too hard." She would groan in reply. Nothing came to mind that she felt was really right.

One afternoon when Godfrey, who was driving a cab for a living, stopped by, she fell into his arms in tears. He heard her out and made a suggestion. Why didn't they let the performers do what they were best at, individual numbers out of black traditions? She could write some skits and some introductions, but what would serve their purpose best would be a revue, a series of separate sketches and songs that featured different artists. Maya saw it at once. She had the title before Godfrey got back to his cab. "We'll call it *Freedom Cabaret*," she shouted across the street to him.

Together Maya and Godfrey produced, directed, and performed in *Freedom Cabaret*. It ended with the entire cast asking the audience to join in "Lift every voice and sing...," the black national anthem that had saved Maya's eighth-grade graduation. The performers worked for minimum wage to raise as much money as possible for the SCLC. Some performers even signed their paychecks over to the cause. The SCLC made money but the cast was without jobs when the performance was over. When the show closed they went back to being elevator operators, waitresses, or cab drivers.

When Maya got a call from the SCLC some months later, she assumed it had to do with closing the books on *Freedom Cabaret*. She was stunned when they told her that Bayard Rustin, the coordinator of SCLC for the New York area, was leaving and he thought she would make a good replacement. He had been impressed with her organizational skills in putting on the show. "I can't type," she reminded them in amazement. They said that wasn't a problem, since she would have a secretary. She took the job.

In the course of a conversation with Dr. King one day, Maya mentioned her brother. Bailey, who had never recovered from his wife's death, was in prison for selling stolen goods. King asked where her brother lived, and Maya told him. King's sympathetic response moved Maya deeply: "Never stop loving him and never deny him," King told her.

It was during this period that Maya was introduced to Vusumzi Make, a South African black lawyer who was in exile from his country. He was in New York to petition the United Nations against South Africa's racial policies. Maya met him at the home of friends and was immediately impressed by his articulate arguments, persuasive speech, and courtly manners. He was equally impressed by Maya and began his pursuit of her by winning Guy's approval first.

His work as a black African revolutionary seemed important and honorable to Maya. She didn't think about cultural differences that might divide them, nor

Maya Angelou succeeded Bayard Rustin as the New York area coordinator of SCLC (Southern Christian Leadership Conference).

about the fact that she was once again setting her life, her desires, her creativity aside for a man. Guy liked him and needed a father in his life. When Vus asked her to marry him and go with him to London to attend meetings of the African National Congress (ANC), she said yes. She quit her job with the SCLC to go on a working honeymoon.

While Vus attended meetings of the ANC, Maya had lunch with the delegates' wives. It was clear from the beginning that these women were not going to spend their lunch time together talking about how well their children were doing in school or what they served for dinner the night before. A West Indian journalist, Ruth Thompson, broke the discussion open with some scathing questions: "What are we here for? Why are African women sitting eating, trying to act cute while African men are discussing serious questions and African children are starving. Have we come to London just to convenience our husbands?"

All of the women agreed that women played as important a role in the struggle for freedom and justice as men. Then they began to share stories. One woman, a lawyer from Sierra Leone, told of her imprisonment and torture during her nation's fight against British rule. The other Africans spoke of legendary women in their own countries who had outsmarted their oppressors. Maya contributed the story of Sojourner Truth, an ex-slave who fought to free her people. Maya writes that on that afternoon in London, she "was in Africa surrounded by her gods and in league with her daughters."

Her newfound sisterhood with African women was quickly buried as Vus took command again when it was time for them to leave England. He told Maya that when she got back to New York, she was to find and furnish a suitable apartment for an African leader. When Vus returned to the United States, he found her choices in furniture too modest and redid the apartment in a grander style. He reminded Maya that she was an African wife now and must keep a proper home for him. With some foreboding Maya withdrew into her housework, even giving up her weekly meetings with the Harlem Writers Guild.

Maya tried to keep a part of her life for herself, but she writes, "heavy lids closed my eyes and the best reading of the best writing could not hold my exhausted attention." In place of her own interests, Maya tried to be an active part of Vus's. She would try to listen to the intense political discussions that took place in her house, but her domestic chores usually prevented her from being present while they were going on. Her sense of independence was threatened, but she loved Vus and thought his work important.

Shortly after she returned to New York, Maya was offered a part in an all-black, off-Broadway production of Jean Genet's play, *The Blacks*. This was a chance for her to get out from under her oppressive housework and regain some of her independence. But she found the Frenchman's bitter, absurdist drama very disturbing. It portrayed blacks winning their struggle against their white oppressors only to become as vicious and oppressive themselves when they came to power.

Maya didn't think black people were like that. She felt they had learned humanity through their suffering that would prevent their ever becoming as evil as whites. Maya saw blacks as much more forgiving: "We turned other cheeks so often our heads seemed to revolve on the end of our necks like old stop-and-go signs....We forgave as if forgiving was our talent."

To Maya, the play was a white foreigner's idea of a people he did not understand. Her friend Max Roach, the musician who was originally to score the play, however, thought it a significant play and urged Maya to reconsider it. Maya mentioned the opportunity to Vus. His first reaction was fury that she would even consider going on stage now that she was his wife. She bristled under Vus's control. "For years before I met Vus," she writes, "my rent had been paid and my son and I had eaten and been clothed by money I made working on stages. When I gave Vus my body and loyalty, I hadn't included all the rights to my life...." She did not like Genet's play particularly, but she

SHOWBILL
THE BLACKS

Jean Genet's stylized play, *The Blacks*, was a bitter indictment of
the racial tensions between blacks and whites.

"chafed under Vus' attitude of total control." Vus, after reading the play, changed his mind and told Maya he thought she should do it.

It was an all-star black cast: James Earl Jones, Roscoe Lee Brown, Godfrey Cambridge, Cicely Tyson, and Lou Gossett, Jr., among others. Maya played the white queen in a white mask and was able to draw on all the meanness she had seen in white women since her early days in Stamps to make her role convincing.

To Maya's amazement, the audiences who packed the theater were not blacks. They were whites, many of whom came back over and over. People would wait for the cast after the show to congratulate them, but when Maya tried to probe their attraction to the play, they got huffy. It became clear that they did not have black friends or neighbors; the ideas in the play were abstractions that moved them but did not relate to their real lives.

Maya quit the play before it closed because of a dispute with Genet over money that he owed her. This left her once again chained to her role as housewife. She was not happy with this role, nor was she pleased with the widening gulf separating her from Guy. Vus had largely taken her place. Guy no longer sought her advice but consulted Vus. They seemed to share little secrets of which she was not privy. She writes, "It was what I said I wanted, but I had to admit to myself that for my son I had become only a reliable convenience. A something of very little importance."

Her being shut out of a close relationship with Guy and her lack of control over her life became almost unbearable when she began getting threatening phone calls. Living with an African revolutionary had its grimmer side. Maya began getting anonymous calls when she was alone in the apartment, telling her that Vus was dead or captured. She would then call everywhere she could think Vus might be to track him down and be sure he was safe. Vus said it was probably the South African security police trying to scare her and to pay no attention. But how could she pay no attention? One morning a woman's voice told her that Guy was in Mid-Town Hospital in the emergency room. She grabbed a taxi and raced to the hospital in terror. They had no record of her son's being admitted, so she finally called his school. He was in history class. It was another cruel hoax.

Added to the constant harassment was Maya's certainty that Vus was seeing another woman. She confronted him, but he denied it and told her, "You are my wife. That is all you need to know."

What seemed to be the final blow to their marriage was the arrival of an eviction notice. They were told they had to leave their apartment within twenty-four hours or be evicted. Vus's pride had prevented him from telling Maya that they were heavily in debt. His response when Maya told him that within a few hours they would be in the streets was "Don't worry about it." Vus left the apartment and returned late that night to inform Maya that he had sold the furniture, rented a furnished apartment, and they were all going to Egypt.

Vus left for Africa immediately. Maya and Guy stayed in a dingy hotel apartment for three weeks and then went to San Francisco. Maya writes, "I needed to see my mother. I needed to be told just one more time that life was what you make of it, and that every tub ought to sit on its own bottom." Instead of finding support from Vivian, Maya ended up taking care of her mother. Vivian had married again but this time it was to an alcoholic. Maya was almost relieved when Vus wired her and Guy their tickets to Cairo.

Maya and the single biggest influence on her life —her mother,
Vivian Baxter Wilburn.

CHAPTER 7

ROOTS

There was much to cry for, much to mourn, but in my heart I felt exalted knowing there was much to celebrate. Although separated from our languages, our families and customs, we had dared to continue to live. We had crossed the unknowable oceans in chains and had written its mystery into "Deep river, my home is over Jordan." Through the centuries of despair and dislocation, we had been creative, because we faced down death by daring to hope.
—Maya Angelou

Africa did not disappoint Maya and Guy. The first two years they spent in Cairo were filled with exotic sights and sounds and exciting international politics. Later, in West Africa, they would taste, see, hear, and feel their ancient heritage and exalt in it. The experience, however, was not without some pain and confusion. Although they claimed their ancestry, their direct roots still lay in the country they loved and hated.

Maya had left the United States as the country was entering a period of social upheaval. In 1963 a church in Birmingham was bombed, killing four children. Civil rights worker Medgar Evers was slain in front of his home in Mississippi. President Kennedy was assassinated in Dallas, Texas. In the following years, racial strife would sweep across the country. Hundreds of years of injustice exploded into riots in Newark, Chicago, Detroit, and Los Angeles.

Maya was literally worlds away from this turmoil. In Cairo, she and Guy reveled in seeing so many brown-skinned people in positions of power and respectability. Guy thrived in school, picking up the Arabic language easily. Maya made friends with several black African diplomatic wives and did not mind being a housewife and hostess—at least not at first.

As Vus began to travel more and more, Maya became more restless. Her desire to have some life of her own, however, turned into a necessity when she learned that they were deeply in debt again. She was determined to get a job.

Maya appealed to David DuBois, a black American newspaper correspondent who had befriended her. David quickly found her an important editorial post on a weekly English-language magazine called *Arab Observer*. She would be the editor for African affairs.

She was both happy and horrified. She had never been a reporter or an editor, and it was Vus who knew about African affairs, not she. She writes that it was as if she "had fallen into a deep trench with steep muddy sides." She wanted desperately to go to the American Embassy and use their library to bone up before the job started, but her radical politics had made her unwelcome there. Once again, she had to dig down into her own resources. As a young, teenage mother, she had bluffed her way into a job as a Creole cook. Now, she had to step into yet another unknown and pretend she knew what she was doing.

She was also scared to tell Vus what she had done. In his culture, a wife that worked was humiliating, and he would be angry that she had taken a job without consulting him first. Maya was finally able to convince Vus that her working would free up more money for his work with political exiles and refugees, which was badly needed. He couldn't deny that. He finally agreed to help her in her work, and in the end they became respectful colleagues.

Despite her inexperience, Maya learned her job quickly. She wrote news stories and editorials and learned how to lay out a story graphically. Later she wrote stories for Radio Cairo and read them on the air. She felt productive again and gained a measure of her old independence.

With her job giving her a renewed sense of self, Maya began to question her marriage to Vus. She knew he was having affairs with other women. At first he tried to cajole her, saying that she was his first wife and he loved her above anyone else. After that didn't work, he explained that he was an African man and that he was entitled to more than one woman. It was a cultural difference that Maya would not accept. Maya knew that their marriage was over. When Guy graduated from high school, Maya was ready to move on, and Vus was ready for her to move on.

She and Guy agreed that the University of Ghana, the pride of a newly independent black country, would be an exciting place for him to get his college education. The whole idea of a black country run by black people for black people was something Maya had to see and experience for herself. The plan was for Maya to take Guy to Accra to get him settled. Then she would travel on to Liberia, where she had lined up a job through her diplomatic friends in Cairo.

When they first arrived in Accra, the capital of Ghana, they walked through the streets and laughed. It was as if the tightly coiled spring that had been their lives in a white society was suddenly released. They marveled at the everyday experience of living in a black country–black policemen, black professors, black bureaucrats, black businessmen.

Two days after their arrival, Guy broke his neck in an automobile accident. With Guy's life hanging in the balance, Maya sunk into depression. The black American community in Accra gave Maya their support and sustained her through her vigil at Guy's bedside. Julian Mayfield, a friend from the Harlem Writers Guild who was in Ghana at the time, saw to it that she met the head of the university theater department. Maya was offered an administrative job with a professor and the use of a house for three months while the owners were away.

Guy slowly recovered and, after recuperating at home, Maya enrolled him in the university. She was suddenly alone. Waiting for feelings of loneliness, instead she remembers thinking, "At last, I'll be able to eat the whole breast of roast chicken by myself."

Maya was welcomed into the black American community. This group of expatriates was searching for a way to define themselves as Africans. The closest Maya came to feeling her heritage directly was actually due to a misunderstanding. One day when Maya could no longer stand the noise and congestion of the city, she decided to explore the countryside. She had a working knowledge of the Fanti language and so felt comfortable exploring unfamiliar places where it was unlikely anyone knew English or any other European language.

At the town of Cape Coast, she stopped for gas. She knew of the reputation of this town. The Cape Coast castle had been the place the Africans were held before they were put on slave ships and taken to America. Many Americans went to see the castle. Maya wanted to avoid it and the horrible history it represented. But, as she says, "history invaded" her car. She knew that if she didn't examine this history, she would never be truly free from it:

> I allowed shapes to come to my imagination: children passed tied together by ropes and chains, tears abashed, stumbling in dull exhaustion, then women, hair uncombed, bodies gritted with sand, and sagging in defeat. Men, muscles without memory, minds dimmed, plodding, leaving bloodied footprints in the dirt....These were the legions, sold by sisters, stolen by brothers, bought by strangers, enslaved by the greedy and betrayed by history.

As the scenes in her mind became fainter, Maya stopped crying.

She continued toward her destination, Dunkwa, a gold-mining town. When she reached the town, she made the acquaintance of some of the local people who mistook her for a Bambara woman from Liberia. Maya writes:

> Because they had taken such relish in detecting my tribal origin I couldn't tell them that they were wrong. Or, less admirably, at that moment I didn't want to remember that I was an American. For the first time since my arrival, I was very nearly home. Not a Ghanaian, but at least accepted as an African. The sensation was worth a lie.

Maya's experience in Dunkwa assured her that despite the terrible history that lay between her and the land of her ancestors, there was still some small part of her that was recognizably African.

Back in Accra, Maya continued to struggle with her dual identity. She and the other black Americans knew that the Ghanaians had not stretched out their arms for their long lost brothers and sisters. They were too busy with their own concerns. Even if the Americans had wanted it to be, Africa was not their home.

The roots that drew the black Americans together lay across the Atlantic. People in the group never spoke of homesickness, but there were shared times that brought memories of home dangerously close to the surface. In an amusing anecdote in her autobiography, Maya tells about the time Julian Mayfield received a shipment of pork from the United States. His friends, including Maya, descended on his house. "We chewed the well-spiced pork of America," Maya writes, "but in fact, we were ravenously devouring Houston and Macon, Little Rock and St. Louis. Our faces eased with sweet delight as we swallowed Harlem and Chicago's south side." Maya realized that out of oppression, a vibrant, black American culture had risen. They loved this rich culture and hated the racism that created it.

In the spring of 1963, this shared culture and history also brought them together as they heard news reports of riots in Birmingham, Alabama, and of Dr. King's arrest. They also knew that a march on Washington was planned for June 20. Although many in the group did not agree with Martin Luther King, Jr.'s non-violent tactics, they felt that they needed to make a statement as black Americans. They planned their own march on the U.S. Embassy in Accra.

The march was held at midnight because of the seven-hour time difference. Maya and the other organizers were surprised at the number of people who turned out. People carried lighted torches as they silently walked toward the embassy. During the march, word came that Dr. W.E.B. DuBois had died. DuBois had been one of the founders of the NAACP— a brilliant and spirited leader in the struggle for civil rights. After becoming disillusioned with the United States, he had emigrated to Ghana, where he spent his last years. Upon hearing of his death, the marchers began to sing:

Oh, Oh Freedom,
Oh, Oh Freedom
Oh, Oh Freedom over me.
And before I'd be a slave
I'd be buried in my grave
And go home to my Lord and be free.

As the morning dawned, the marchers approached the
U.S. Embassy. Two Marines came out to raise the
American flag. One of them was black. The crowd
called to the soldier to join them. But he ignored them,
and with the white soldier unfolded the flag. As they
raised it Maya realized,

> Many of us had only begun to realize in Africa that the Stars
> and Stripes was our flag and our only flag, and that knowl-
> edge was almost too painful to bear. We could physically
> return to Africa, find jobs, learn languages, even marry and
> remain on African soil all our lives, but we were born in the
> United States which had rejected, enslaved, exploited, then
> denied us....
>   I shuddered to think that while we wanted that flag
> dragged into the mud and sullied beyond repair, we also
> wanted it pristine, its white stripes, summer cloud white.
> Watching it wave in the breeze…made us nearly choke with
> emotion. It lifted us up with its promise and broke our hearts
> with its denial.

Malcolm X's visit to Accra also opened Maya's thinking. In the United States, Malcolm X was a black
leader who disagreed with Martin Luther King, Jr.'s
nonviolent, love-will-conquer-all philosophy.
Malcolm had been a follower of Elijah Muhammad,
who had denounced whites as "blue-eyed devils" and
claimed that the white race was intent on black geno-
cide. When Maya and the other black Americans in
Ghana saw Malcolm, he had just returned from a
pilgrimage to the Islamic holy city of Mecca. He
shocked his audience when he said that he no longer
believed that all white people were evil. In Mecca, he

Malcolm X was a mesmerizing speaker who preached that blacks must defend themselves against the violence of white racism.

said, "I met White men with blue eyes who I can call brother with conviction." After Malcolm X left Ghana, Maya writes that his "presence had elevated us, but with his departure, we were what we had been before: a little group of black folks, looking for a home."

Maya's feeling of being torn between Africa and America was not helped by the realization that her son was a grown man who she had little, if any, control over. Suspicion became fact when she learned that he was dating a woman from the U.S. embassy who was old enough to be his mother. After a showdown between them, where Guy informed his mother that his life was his own to live, Maya decided that she had to get away from Ghana, Guy, and, as she puts it, "the situation."

When an offer came to join the original cast of the play, *The Blacks*, Maya grabbed it. She spent several months traveling through Germany and Italy and returned to Africa via Cairo. After renewing her friendship with David DuBois and others, she returned to Ghana and to her son. In her absence, Guy had matured into the man he said he was before she left.

Guy explained to his mother that he appreciated all that she had done for him, that she had been a good mother to him, but now his life belonged to him. Maya knew that all of the previous departures had been rehearsals for this final scene. She felt set adrift for a while, but soon regained her own life. It helped that Malcolm X had approached Maya with an offer to work for the Organization of Afro-American Unity in New York. Now, with a job in hand and with Guy safely launched into adulthood, Maya felt ready to return to the United States.

Africa had given Maya's life greater meaning and understanding, but the United States was where she belonged. Like two giant tap roots, America and Africa were intertwined in her life. Her mind, her imagination, and her heart would now spread like the huge limbs of the baobab tree.

In *All God's Children Need Traveling Shoes*, another volume of her autobiography, Maya writes:

> I had seen the African moon grow red as fire over the black hills at Aburi and listened to African priests implore God in rhythm and voices which carried me back to Calvary Baptist Church in San Francisco.
>
> If the heart of Africa still remained illusive, my search for it had brought me closer to understanding myself and other human beings. The ache for home lives in all of us, the safe place where we can go as we are and not be questioned. It impels mighty ambitions and dangerous capers....Hoping that by doing these things, home will find us acceptable or failing that, that we all forget our awful yearning for it.

Maya Angelou in 1970, at the publication of the first volume of her autobiography.

CHAPTER 8

DO WHAT THE SPIRIT SAY DO

*Maya's story conveys a deep mythological truth about suffering
and redemption, about the journey a person takes into the
experience and knowledge of self, where any potential gift
anyone has to share with the world lies waiting to be discovered.*
—Bill Moyers

The fifth, and latest, volume of Maya's autobiography, *All God's Children Need Traveling Shoes*, ends with her returning to the United States. For the past twenty years, Maya has kept a tight control on the personal details of her life. She once commented to an interviewer, "I will say how old I am [53 at the time]. I will say how tall I am, but I will not say how many times I have been married." So until Maya is ready to tell what she wants us to know about her, we must be satisfied with only a hazy picture of what her private life has been like.

We do know that when she returned from Africa, she settled in Los Angeles and supported herself by writing screenplays, acting, and lecturing. We also know that by the early 1970s, she had moved to north-ern California, settling first in Berkeley and then in Sonoma County. Guy by this time had also returned to the United States and had become the first black execu-tive with Western Airlines.

In 1973, she married again. Her husband was Paul du Feu, a writer and cartoonist and former husband of feminist activist Germaine Greer. Maya and du Feu were divorced in 1981.

In 1982, a lifetime chair in American culture was endowed at Wake Forest University in Winston-Salem, North Carolina, where Maya had once been a visiting professor. With her high school diploma and a hatful of honorary doctorates from colleges and universities all over the United States, Maya was asked to fill this important professorship. She agreed—with the stipu-lation that for the first three years she would teach only one semester and use the rest of her time for writing.

One wonders why she chose the South to settle in, a place full of so much painful history. In a recent radio interview, she explains what drew her back:

> A number of Northerners and Westerners and
> Easterners…simply don't know the beauty of the South
> otherwise they would not wonder why people risk their lives
> when fighting to hold it, to earn it, to claim it. The South is
> gorgeous.
> I also wanted to hear the voices, the sounds of Black southern
> voices and white southern voices when they are not filled
> with hate. I wanted to go South because there is less hypoc-
> risy.

Perhaps it is fitting that we know so little about Maya's recent personal life. Certainly, after revealing, some-times in painful detail, forty years of her life, she de-serves some privacy. But more importantly, this lack of information makes us focus on her working life, on what she has accomplished as an artist—it is a breathtaking view of the talents of a creative and prodigious woman.

Maya's early lectures in the late 1960s and early 1970s were part of the black consciousness movement that was sweeping the nation. With the assassination of Martin Luther King, Jr., in 1968, blacks needed people who could speak about black cultural contributions to American society. Maya, along with many others, was able to translate black experience and reveal its richness. At the University of California at Los Angeles (UCLA), she articulated the blacks' contributions to American culture. In 1970, Maya began to focus on the "mythical black woman" and her position in black and white society. "The black American female," Maya said, "has nursed a nation of strangers—literally. And has remained compassionate. This, to me, is survival. She is strong. And she is inclusive, as opposed to exclusive. She has included all the rest of humanity in her life and has often been excluded from their lives. I'm very impressed with her."

These lectures, however, were not Maya's main endeavor. Play and screenwriting were taking up most of her creative energies. One of Maya's earliest and most successful writing projects was the screenplay *Georgia, Georgia* (1972). The story is about a black singer who tours Sweden and becomes fascinated by the white culture. Her companion, another black woman, angrily counters her friend's attraction to white society. Maya wrote the play as an attempt to portray black women as they really are.

She has also spread her writing talents into television. In 1968, National Educational Television in San Francisco produced a ten-show series she wrote called *Black, Blues, Black,* which shows how African cultural traditions have influenced American life. Maya combined music, dance, drama, and narrative to show viewers how strongly African culture has permeated our daily lives. For example, in one program she traces common children's games such as jacks, patti-cake, and tag back to their African origins.

Sister, Sister was a major television program Maya did for NBC in 1978. The two-hour program was a milestone for blacks in television because it was drama. There were comedy programs that featured blacks, but there was no serious drama at the time.

In *Sister, Sister*, Maya was struggling to counter the stereotypical image of blacks. She angrily pointed out in one newspaper interview that black women are usually "either the hot mulatto or the mammy." She added, "I don't know where casting agents go to...find all those small, black children who are sassy and rude and brutish, all those young men who grin all the time, can't stand up straight, and can speak neither standard English or good black English." In portraying three sisters from a middle-class family, Maya was attempting to show complex black characters. She maintained that portraying blacks as either thugs or saints was just another kind of discrimination.

For some unknown reason, *Sister, Sister* was put on hold. Many television critics asked why a show that was completed and that got good reviews was not being shown. Some felt that racist attitudes were delaying its broadcast; others believed that NBC was just getting nervous about breaking new programming ground in showing black drama. *Sister, Sister* was finally aired in 1982.

Acting, playwriting, and screenwriting engaged Maya's time. She appeared in a stage production of the Greek tragedy *Medea* (1966) in Hollywood, and in 1972 made her Broadway debut in the two-character play *Look Away*. In the play, Maya plays Mary Todd Lincoln's dressmaker. The play was not a success—it closed the same night it opened, but reviewers raved

Maya Angelou and her son, Clyde.

about Maya's performance. And in 1977, she played
Kunta Kinte's grandmother in the TV series based on
Alex Haley's book *Roots*.

Despite Maya's varied and prolific creative life, she
still needed to give a clearer voice to the black
woman's experience. It was her old friend James
Baldwin and cartoonist-playwright Jules Feiffer who
challenged her to write her own story. Maya would
often entertain her friends with anecdotes about her
growing up. Both Baldwin and Feiffer told her that she
must tell her story on paper—just as she had told it to
them—without losing any of the flavor or humor.
Here, they felt, was an authentic vision of black life
through a woman's eyes.

Maya began writing *I Know Why the Caged Bird Sings*
in the late 1960s. She knew that if she did not tell it
honestly, it would not ring true to blacks or whites.
She had to face her own mistakes and relive painful
experiences—she could not lie or soften the harsh
truths.

Maya was following a well-established, black literary tradition when she chose autobiography as the
form she would use to tell her story. Narratives like

that of Frederick Douglass vividly exposed the cruel-
ties of slavery. Later writers such as James Weldon
Johnson at the turn of the century and Richard Wright
in the 1940s used autobiography to express the pain,
joy, and richness of black life in the United States.
Fictional autobiographies such as Richard Wright's
Native Son and Ralph Ellison's *Invisible Man* took black
literature into the American cultural mainstream.

I Know Why the Caged Bird Sings came out in 1970.
The reviews were stunning. *Newsweek* said the book
"regularly throws out rich, dazzling images which
delight and surprise with their simplicity." The review
went on to say that the book was more than a mere feat
of skill or ingenuity, "It quietly and gracefully portrays
and pays tribute to the courage, dignity, and endur-
ance of the small, rural community in which she spent
most of her early years...." The good opinion of the
press was important to Maya, and it helped put the
book on the national best-seller list, but the opinion of
her black peers meant more to her.

Her friend and fellow writer James Baldwin was not
disappointed in the work he had urged her to take on:

> *I Know Why the Caged Bird Sings* liberates the reader into life
> simply because Maya Angelou confronts her own life with
> such moving wonder, such a luminous dignity. I have no
> words for this achievement, but I know that not since the days
> of my childhood, when the people in books were more real
> than the people one saw every day, have I found myself so
> moved.... Her portrait is a Biblical study of life in the midst
> of death.

Throughout the next 16 years, Maya, as one reviewer
noted, produced a "stunning succession" of books
about her life: *Gather Together in My Name* (1974),
Singin' and Swingin' and Gettin' Merry Like Christmas
(1976), *The Heart of a Woman* (1981), and finally, *All
God's Children Need Traveling Shoes* (1986). One critic

has commented that "the entire autobiography… is a tribute to the author's strong faith, personal courage, talent, and thoroughgoing sense of self-worth."

Maya tells a genuine story with powerful and rhythmic language. And few would disagree that her books are a wellspring of insight. She has compressed black American reality into hard nuggets of experience that on one level give the reader an understanding of black life, and on another level a greater understanding of human beings in general.

One measure of the enduring worth of Maya Angelou's work is that colleges and universities across the country use her autobiographies in American studies and women studies courses. Her accessibility as a writer and her sharp observations of what life is like for a black woman in this country make it possible for students to get a rare look into black America. Many critics feel, in fact, that *I Know Why the Caged Bird Sings* has already become a classic.

With the success of *I Know Why the Caged Bird Sings*, Maya was able to begin publishing her poetry. Since 1971, she has published six volumes of her poems. Her latest book, *I Shall Not Be Moved*, was published in 1990. Many people feel that Maya's greatest strength as a writer lies in her prose, not her poetry. Her best poems use the speech patterns and rhythms of the black culture and contain the same energy and liveliness that her prose does. An example of this is the poem "When I Think About Myself," which is about a black cleaning woman:

Sixty years in these folk's world
The child I works for calls me girl
I say "Yes ma'am" for working sake.
Too proud to bend
Too poor to break,
I laugh until my stomach ache
When I think about myself

Sassiness is another prominent characteristic of Maya's poems, as seen in "And Still I Rise":

> Does my haughtiness offend you?
> Don't you take it awful hard
> 'Cause I laugh like I've got gold mines
> Diggin' in my own backyard.

Many critics feel that Maya's poetry can only be truly appreciated when it is read aloud by the poet herself. Her dramatic talents bring out the tension and sharp cadences in the poems, which the silent printed words cannot begin to convey.

Moving from college to college and from film project to theater project makes Maya something of a vagabond. A play might take her to one city for several months and a writer-in-residence stint requires her to move into another environment. There is only one constant: her autobiographical writing and her poetry goes with her wherever she is.

When Maya is in the middle of a writing project she works for long stretches of time. There can be no distractions. This is so important, in fact, that she takes a hotel room in whatever town she happens to be in and tells the management not to disturb her. She assures them that she is not using the bed, so they needn't worry about changing the sheets. She stocks the room with a dictionary, a Bible, a Roget's Thesaurus, and a bottle of sherry. She arrives at the room at 5:30 A.M. and works without a break until at least one or two in the afternoon. She might begin writing again after dinner and continue into the night. She does this day after day until the project is finished. At one hotel the management slipped a note under her door, which read: "Ms. Angelou, please let us get in there and change the sheets. We think they are moldy." But even these pleas did not move her.

As with many writers, Maya has many self-doubts. "Once I get into the room and look at the yellow pad, I am absolutely terrified," she says. "I think: I have talked a good talk. I have fooled everybody. Everybody thinks I can write." Her books, however, testify to her success in overcoming these fears.

Maya is not a snob about being an artist. In fact she often takes great pains to bring an understanding of art into people's lives, to demystify it. " I very much dislike those 'artists' with the '-e' on the end." She has explained in the past, "They're terribly mysterious and strange and inapproachable, and they go around with the back of their fists glued to their forehead. It's so phony....You don't have to do that. You really can live lovely lives and do your work, even as a grocer does his work, and not always bring it right into the center of the living room for everybody else to have to deal with." During a recent Oprah Winfrey show, Maya compared the art of writing to doing anything well. "It is no more magical than the art of laying bricks or...running a family with some grace and some charm and some laughter and some love."

In an interview on National Public Radio, Maya was asked what she wanted to do next with her life after being a dancer, actress, singer, poet, and writer. Her response was characteristically Maya:

> The truth is, my truth is that I'm really trying to play it good. I'm trying to be a great writer. And maybe more importantly a great human being....It means being fair. To be merciful. It is one thing to be gentle if you are weak but to be very strong and to be gentle...it doesn't get much better than that.

Maya Angelou—singer, dancer, writer, composer, poet, lecturer, editor, movie director, and cable car conductor.

CONCLUSION

A BOLD WANDERER

Why do we journey, muttering
like rumors among the stars?
—Maya Angelou
From the poem, "Is Love"

Being born into a white, racist, male-dominated society, Maya had three strikes against her from the moment of her birth: she was poor, black, and female. Coming from a broken family and having a child at sixteen years of age made her chances slim of ever having a normal, decent life—let alone an exceptional life—almost nonexistent. So how did Marguerite Ann Johnson, poor black girl from the South, become Maya Angelou, actress, dancer, singer, songwriter, playwright, and renowned author?

Certainly, her journey as a creative person was uncharted, unplanned. Unlike some artists, it cannot be said that at some point in her childhood she knew she wanted to be a writer and so set out to become one.

But there are a few signposts one can spot that tell us something about Maya as a creative person.

One of these signposts is Maya's boldness. As a young woman, she was not a well-prepared tourist who knew beforehand what to expect along the road. She was a free-spirited wanderer. Not only did she not always know where she was headed or where she would end up, but she often took off across unknown territory. Her decision to run away from her father and her time with the street children, her decision to find out what sex was all about, and her bluffing her way into almost every job she took from Creole cooking to becoming R.L. Poole's dance partner are all times in her life when she took on the unknown. Some of these decisions led to positive things (a career in show business, a job as a street car conductor) and some led her to the brink of disaster (her rush into unsuitable relationships with men). But as she matured she sorted out what was good for her and what was harmful. Her willingness to tackle the unknown, however, remained and allowed her to pursue her creative impulses.

Audaciousness without intelligence, of course, is just recklessness. Fortunately, Maya was endowed with a good mind. She learned from her mistakes and kept pulling herself up, even when the situation was dragging her down. When she had to take a job in a sleazy nightclub, she refused to use sexually suggestive gimmicks in her performance. She was a dancer who could dance and who wanted to give even this unsavory audience something of quality.

She also gobbled up knowledge wherever she found it. Even in the worst of times, she found time to read. Her creative energies drove her to take dance lessons after long hours as a cook or waitress. Her natural ability to absorb knowledge is almost mythical. She has an uncanny talent for picking up speech patterns and whole languages (she speaks five fluently). This gift has served her well as a dramatist, actress, and writer. Her descriptive powers have also given her writing a sharp-edged authenticity. Scenes from her childhood in Arkansas and from her life in Africa are especially vivid.

Maya would probably be the first one to say that she did not get where she is today by herself. At least three people profoundly influenced her life—Annie Henderson, Mrs. Flowers, and Vivian Johnson—and contributed to Maya's creative life in some way. Her grandmother, Annie Henderson, gave her life a moral and ethical context and the rich connection to black culture—both African and American. Mrs. Flowers opened the doors of learning and language. And her mother, Vivian Johnson, gave her the confidence to take on whatever challenge came her way—"Can't never did anything," as her mother used to say.

Maya's creativity has also been nourished with elements of both white and black culture. She had an insatiable appetite for good literature even as a young girl. James Weldon Johnson as well as William Shakespeare fed her already fertile imagination. The black community has, of course, been the main meal for Maya. It has given her spiritual sustenance and been the rich source for her writing.

Two people may be presented with the same set of circumstances, but it is the person who dares to explore and who has the ability to translate the possible meaning of the events for others who is creative. Maya has taken her life as a black American and looked at it with honesty and insight and given us a true and compelling picture not only of the black community but of the human condition.

CHRONOLOGY

1928	Marguerite Johnson born April 4, St. Louis, Missouri.
1939	*World War II begins.*
1940	Graduated from Lafayette Training School, Stamps, Arkansas.
1941	*Japan attacks Pearl Harbor, Hawaii; U.S. enters World War II.*
1944	Maya works as a conductor on the San Francisco cable cars.
1945	*World War II ends.* Graduated from Mission High School, San Francisco. Son Clyde (Guy) Johnson born.
1950	*Korean War begins.*
1953	Began performing at the Purple Onion in San Francisco. *Korean War ends.*
1954	*Brown v. Board of Education.*
1954–1955	Toured Europe with *Porgy and Bess* company for the U.S. State Department.
1955	Montgomery, Alabama, bus boycott.
1956	*Dwight D. Eisenhower elected president.*
1957	*Civil Rights Bill passes.* Records "Miss Calypso" album for Liberty Records. *The founding of the Southern Christian Leadership Council, headed by Dr. Martin Luther King, Jr. Governor Orval Faubus of Arkansas prevents nine black children from enrolling in an all-white school.*
1960	*Civil Rights Act 1960; John F. Kennedy elected president.* Produces, directs, and appears in *Freedom Cabaret* and Genet's play, *The Blacks*.

Nonviolent Coordinating Committee formed.

1961   *Freedom Rides.*
Northeastern regional coordinator for Southern Christian Leadership Conference.

1962   Associate editor, *Arab Observer*, Cairo.
U.S. enters war with Vietnam.

1963   *Birmingham church bombed, killing four children.*
March on Washington.
Medgar Evers killed.
President Kennedy killed.

1963–   Assistant administrator at the School of
1965   Music and Drama, University of Ghana.
Feature editor for the *African Review,* and contributor to the *Ghanaian Times* and Ghanaian Broadcasting Company.

1964   *Lyndon B. Johnson elected president.*
Martin Luther King, Jr. awarded the Nobel Peace Prize.
Freedom summer.

1965   *Malcolm X killed.*
Watts riot in Los Angeles.
Voting Rights Act.

1966   *The Least of These,* a two-act drama produced in Los Angeles.
Acted in stage version of *Medea* in Hollywood.

1968   *Martin Luther King, Jr. assassinated.*
Blacks, Blues, Black airs.
Recorded "The Poetry of Maya Angelou," for GWP Records.

1970   *I Know Why the Caged Bird Sings,* the first book in her autobiographical series.
Nominated for the National Book Award.
Writer-in-residence at University of Kansas.
Granted a Yale University fellowship.

1971	Publishes *Just Give Me a Cool Drink of Water 'fore I Diiie,* first book of poetry.
1972	Nominated for a Pulitzer Prize. *Georgia, Georgia,* a screenplay for Independent Cinerama.
1973	Nominated for a Tony Award for her appearance in *Look Away,* a Broadway play.
1974	Publishes *Gather Together in My Name,* second book in autobiography. Becomes distinguished visiting professor at Wake Forest University, Wichita State University, and California State University. Adapts the play *Ajax,* which is produced in Los Angeles. Writes screenplay *All Day Long* for American Film Institute.
1975	*Oh Pray My Wings Are Gonna Fit Me Well,* second book of poems published. Appointed to the American Revolution Bicentennial Council by President Ford. Works on "Assignment America" series for television. Becomes Rockefeller scholar and goes to Italy. Receives honorary degrees from Smith College and Mills College. **U.S. withdraws from Vietnam.**
1976	Publishes *Singin' and Swingin' and Gettin' Merry Like Christmas,* third book in autobiography. Works on "The Legacy" and "The Inheritors," for television. Chosen Woman of the Year in Communications by the *Ladies' Home Journal.* Receives honorary degree from Lawrence University, Kansas.

1978	Publishes *And Still I Rise*, third book of poems.
1981	Publishes *The Heart of a Woman*, fourth book in autobiography.
1982	Appointed as Chair in American Studies at Wake Forest University, North Carolina. Writes *Sister, Sister*, a teleplay for NBC.
1983	Publishes *Shaker, Why Don't You Sing?*, fourth book of poems.
1986	Publishes *All God's Children Need Traveling Shoes*, fifth book in autobiography.
1987	Publishes *Now Sheba Sings the Song*, fifth book of poems.
1990	Publishes *I Shall Not Be Moved*, sixth book of poems.

SELECTED WORKS

I Know Why the Caged Bird Sings, Random House, 1970.
Just Give Me a Cool Drink of Water 'Fore I Diiie, Random House, 1971.
Gather Together in My Name, Random House, 1974.
Oh, Pray My Wings Are Gonna Fit Me Well, Random House, 1975.
Singin' and Swingin' and Gettin' Merry Like Christmas, Random House, 1976.
And Still I Rise, Random House, 1978.
The Heart of a Woman, Random House, 1981.
Shaker Why Don't You Sing, Random House, 1978.
All God's Children Need Traveling Shoes, Random House, 1986.
Now Sheba Sing the Song, E.P. Dutton, 1987.
I Shall Not Be Moved, Random House, 1990.

GLOSSARY

arabesque In ballet, the extension of one leg straight in back, while the position of arms and body may vary.

baobab tree A tree with a huge trunk and deep roots.

calypso music A style of music that comes from the West Indies and that is marked by lively rhythm. The song lyrics are usually improvised.

chair A special and prestigious teaching position at a college or university.

character sketch A piece of writing that describes the personality of one character.

Cold War The hostility between the United States and the Soviet Union from the late 1940s to 1990.

emotive Appealing to or expressing feelings.

Great Depression The collapse of the world-wide economy from 1929–1939.

Harlem Renaissance A surge of black artistic work stretching from about 1919 to 1929 in Harlem, New York.

melodrama A drama, such as a play, film, or teleplay, that is concerned with exaggerated conflicts and emotions and stereotypical characters.

pantomime Acting without words.

screenplay A script written for a film.

spirituals Religious songs usually of a deeply emotional character that originated in southern black churches.

writer-in-residence A writer at a university or college who is not on the permanent staff but gives special classes in his or her field.

BIBLIOGRAPHY

Angelou, Maya. "Oprah Winfrey," *Ms.*, January/ February 1989.

Benson, C. "Interview with Maya Angelou," *Writer's Digest*, January, 1975.

"The Black Scholar Interviews Maya Angelou," *Black Scholar*, 8 (January-February 1973).

"I Know Why the Caged Bird Sings," *Ebony* 25 (April 1970).

Julianelli, J. "Angelou: Interview," *Harper's Bazaar*, November 1972.

Kent, George E. "Maya Angelou's *I Know Why the Caged Bird Sings* and Black Autobiographical Tradition," *Kansas Quarterly*, 7 (Summer 1975).

Smith, Sidonie Ann. "The Song of a Caged Bird: Maya Angelou's Quest for Self-Acceptance," *Southern Humanities Review* 7 (Fall 1973).

Weller, Sheila. "Work in Progress: Maya Angelou," *Intellectual Digest* 3 (June 1973).

Contemporary Literary Criticism, Gale, Volume XII, 1980, Volume XXXV, 1985.

Dictionary of Literary Biography, Volume XXXVIII: *Afro-American Writers after 1955: Dramatists and Prose Writers*, Gale, 1985.

Creativity, Bill Moyers interviews Maya Angelou in Stamps, Arkansas, 1982. Available for viewing at the Museum of Broadcasting, 1 E. 53 St., New York, NY 10022. Transcript available from Journal Graphics, Inc., 267 Broadway, New York, NY 10007.

The Oprah Winfrey Show, interviews with Maya Angelou and Alice Walker, June 2, 1989. Transcript available from Journal Graphics, Inc., 267 Broadway, New York NY 10007.

INDEX

A

Accra, Ghana, 99-100, 102, 103
Africa, 89, 90, 97-105, 109-110
African National Congress (ANC), 90
*All God's Children Need Traveling
    Shoes* (Angelou), 105, 107
"And Still I Rise" (Angelou),
    114
And Then We Heard Thunder
    (Killens), 81
Angeles, Tosh, 67-68
Angelou, Maya
    in Africa, 7-8, 97-105
    autobiography of, 9, 83, 86,
        102, 105, 107, 111-113
    childhood of, 8-49
    creativity of, 9, 21, 25, 44, 55,
        60, 60, 72, 74-75, 115
    dance and, 21, 40, 42, 45, 59,
        60, 62, 69, 71, 73
    drama and, 40-41, 59, 71, 92-
        94, 109-111
    in Europe, 75-76
    illnesses of, 68, 100
    jobs of, 47-48, 57, 59, 62-62,
        66, 67, 69, 70, 89, 100, 108
    and language, 26, 76, 81-82,
        85-86, 100
    literature and, 19, 27-28, 57-
        59
    marriages of, 67-68, 89-92,
        98-99, 108
    mentors of, 26-27, 40, 85
    music and, 7-8, 15, 25-26, 31-
        32, 60, 70, 71, 75, 80
    name of, 9, 70-71
    parents and, 10, 14-18, 39, 44
    as playwright, 83-84, 87-88,
        109
    poetry and, 28, 75, 82, 113-
        114
    pregnancy of, 49, 51-52
    as professor, 108

racism and, 30-31, 34-35, 37-
    38, 58-59, 76, 102
religion and, 13, 22, 25-26,
    31-32
romances of, 56, 66, 67-68
school and, 32-35, 39-40, 52
self-image of, 9, 14, 46, 55,
    80-81, 83-84, 99, 101-102,
    115
sexual abuse of, 22-23
son and, 53, 55, 57, 62, 63, 66-
    68, 76-77, 79-80, 83, 89, 94,
    98, 99-100, 104-105, 108
street life and, 41-46, 66
television and, 109-111
writing and, 81-86, 98-99,
    109-115
Apollo Theatre, 86
Arab Observer, 98
Army, U.S., 54, 59, 80

B

Baldwin, James, 81, 111, 112
Baxter, Vivian
    children and, 18-22, 46-47,
        67, 95
    grandson and, 55, 59, 76
    health of, 62
    marriages of, 39, 41, 53, 95
Black, Blues, Black (Angelou),
    109
black people
    autobiographies of, 112
    civil rights and, 80, 86-87
    consciousness movement of,
        109
    country for, 99-100, 101-102
    dance and, 21
    jobs for, 8, 12, 41, 53-55
    language of, 43
    music of, 7-8, 14, 25-26, 31-
        32, 70, 86

Photo Credits:

Pages 2, 23: Photofest; 11: Erich Hartman/Magnum Photos; 12, 16: Library of Congress, Walker Evans photograph; 15: Library of Congress, Dorothea Lange photograph; 20, 36, 54, 61: The Bettmann Archive; 24, 42, 46, 81, 82, 90: UPI/Bettmann Newsphotos; 29, 74, 87, 106: Wide World Photos; 30: Eliott Erwitt/Magnum Photos; 50: Schomberg Center for Research in Black Culture, The New York Public Library, Astor, Lenox, and Tilden Foudations, Morgan Smith photograph; 64, 93: Billy Rose Theatre Collection, The New York Public Library at Lincoln Center, Astor, Lenox, and Tilden Foundations; 71: San Francisco Public Library; 78: © Columbia Pictures/Photofest; 84: Freedman/Abeles Collection, The New York Public Library at Lincoln Center, Astor, Lenox, and Tilden Foundations; 96, 111: Mary Ellen Mark photograph; 104: Eve Arnold/Magnum Photos; 116: Wayne Miller/courtesy Life Magazine, © Time Warner, Inc.; **Color Insert:** Page 1: Library, Camera Press London/Globe Photos; 2: *Women's Wear Daily*; 3: Chester Higgins, Jr./New York Times Pictures; 4: Brian Leatart/© Bon Appétit Publishing Corporation, reprinted with permission; 5: Billy Rose Theatre Collection, The New York Public Library at Lincoln Center, Astor, Lenox, and Tilden Foundations; 6: AP/Wide World Photos, courtesy of Spencer Lawrence.
Photo Research: Photosearch, Inc.